Shootdown

A World War II Bomber Pilot's Experience
as a Prisoner of War in Germany

by
William H. Wheeler

Burd Street Press
Shippensburg, Pennsylvania

Copyright © 2002 by William H. Wheeler

ALL RIGHTS RESERVED—No part of this book may be reproduced in any form without permission in writing from the publisher, except by a reviewer who wishes to quote brief passages in connection with a review.

Photograph credits: Courtesy *The Longest Mission*, The Special Collections Branch, United States Air Force Academy Library.

This Burd Street Press publication
was printed by
Beidel Printing House, Inc.
63 West Burd Street
Shippensburg, PA 17257-0708 USA

The acid-free paper used in this book meets the guidelines for permanence and durability of the Committee on Production Guidelines for Book Longevity of the Council on Library Resources.

For a complete list of available publications
please write
Burd Street Press
Division of White Mane Publishing Company, Inc.
P.O. Box 708
Shippensburg, PA 17257-0708 USA

Library of Congress Cataloging-in-Publication Data

Wheeler, William H., 1916-
　Shootdown : a World War II bomber pilot's experience as a prisoner of war in Germany / by William H. Wheeler.
　　p. cm.
　ISBN 1-57249-310-0 (alk. paper)
　1. Wheeler, William H., 1916- 2. World War, 1939-1945--Personal narratives, American. 3. Bomber pilots--United States--Biography. 4. World War, 1939-1945--Prisoners and prisons--Germany. 5. Prisoners of war--United States--Biography. I. Title.

D811.W446 A3 2002
940.54'7243'092--dc21

2002071276

PRINTED IN THE UNITED STATES OF AMERICA

Dedicated to Mary, my loving wife

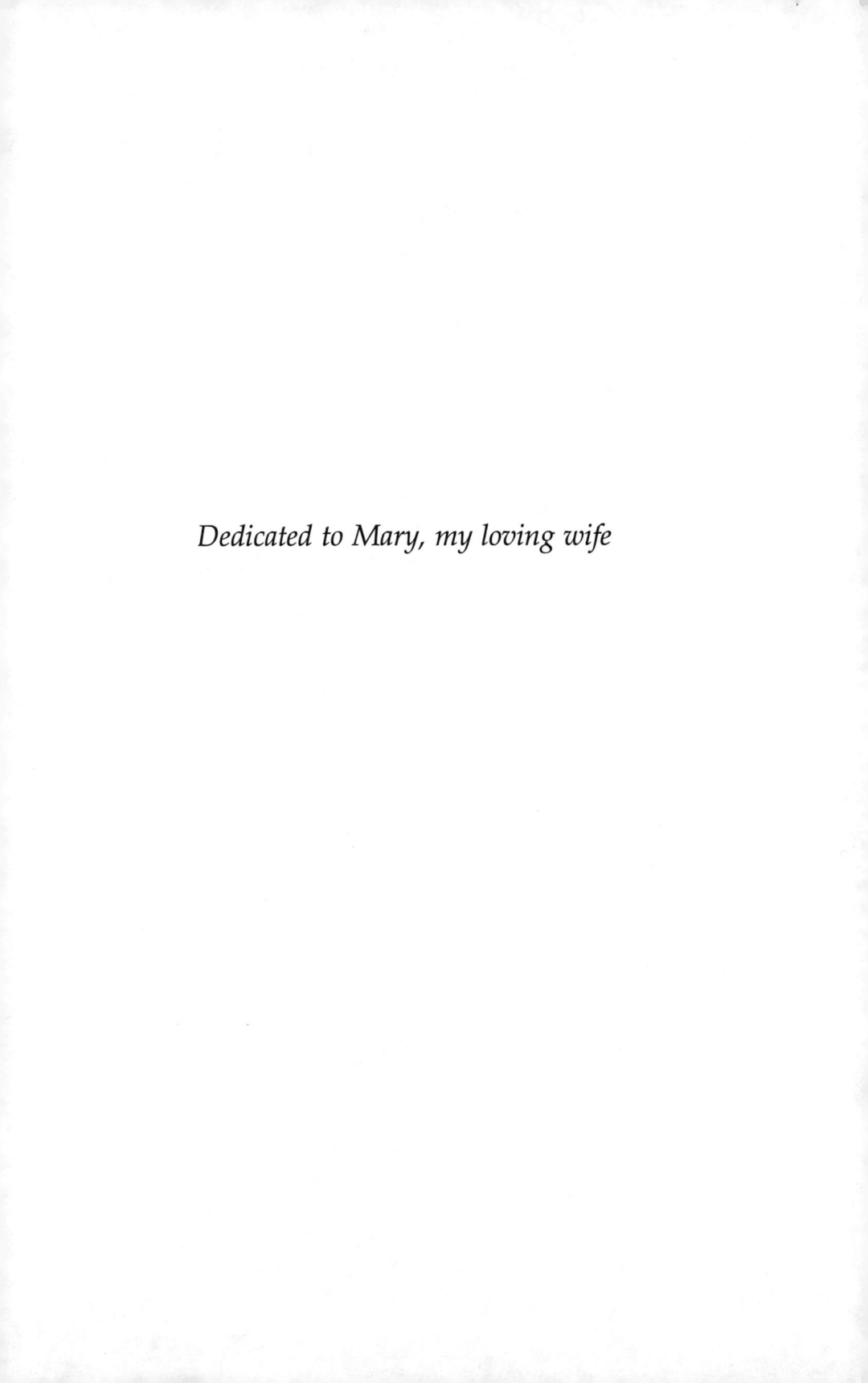

Contents

Acknowledgments vi
"If" vii
Chapter 1 Bail Out 1
Chapter 2 Captured 12
Chapter 3 German Transport 34
Chapter 4 Center Compound 48
Chapter 5 Escape Attempt 58
Chapter 6 First Letters 65
Chapter 7 First Christmas 83
Chapter 8 Senior American Officer (SAO) 90
Chapter 9 Block Commander 95
Chapter 10 Allied Invasion 104
Chapter 11 Summer of '44 113
Chapter 12 Allied Armies Advance 118
Chapter 13 Evacuation 124
Chapter 14 The Long March 128
Chapter 15 Nuremberg 135
Chapter 16 On the Road Again 155
Chapter 17 Liberation 164
Chapter 18 Reunited 175
Chapter 19 Marry Me 188
Chapter 20 The Wedding 196
Chapter 21 Home at Last 207
Epilogue 211

Acknowledgments

The Friends of the Air Force Academy Library, and particularly General Albert P. Clark, for granting me permission to use the photographs in *The Longest Mission*, which enhanced my story immensely.

Laurie Nesbuits, for her outstanding editorial help.

Colonel Arthur A. Durand for his excellent book *Stalag Luft III*.

General Delmar T. Spivey for his superb recollections as written in *POW Odyssey*.

If

If I hadn't had the notion I wanted silver wings,
If I hadn't let emotion blind my eyes to safer things,
If I only had been willing to instruct some other guys,
If I hadn't been so eager to get amid the noise,
If I hadn't been on schedule to fly that certain day,
If I'd only been more careful and kept out of the way,
If fate had only let me be free another night,
If I could have spoken German and said just what was right,
If I only quit my griping and realize just how,
Very, very lucky, I am to be here now.

– From Claudius Belk's Wartime Log
Courtesy Norm Flayderman

Chapter 1

Bail Out

"Lieutenant, we're on fire!" shouted the flight engineer over the intercom.

"Okay, Bayne, hold on." I acknowledged him sharply and called Cobb. "How you doing back there, Jim?"

The radio operator, Jim Cobb, was standing on the catwalk in the bomb bay just forward of the radio compartment, fighting a fire that seemed to intensify with each squirt of the handheld fire extinguisher. The fire had started in number two engine and couldn't be quenched by the engine extinguishers. It had burned through the wing root and into the fuselage. We had to open the bomb bay doors and salvo the bombs to get to the fire. As Cobb emptied a container, Ray Gillet, the waist gunner, handed him another. But it was a futile effort and he finally called the pilot. "Can't put it out with these damn little extinguishers, sir. It's burning like hell and this is the last one we've got back here."

"How about it, Bayne? Can you get to the fire and help Jim?"

Bayne Scurlock, the flight engineer, reached down from his top turret position and grabbed a portable extinguisher. But he was forced back through the turret into the cockpit by the intense heat when he opened the forward hatch leading into the bomb bay. He grabbed me by the shoulder forcing me

1

to turn around, pointing to the fire blazing in the bomb bay and shouted, "SIR, THE FIRE'S OUT OF CONTROL!"

I saw the fierce flames bellowing out of the bomb bay hatch, and knew that we had to abandon our B-17. The oxygen tanks are mounted on the bulkhead just forward of the bomb bay. Reluctantly, I called the crew over the intercom. "Bail out, guys! Get out NOW! She might blow any minute. And . . . good luck." I hit the alarm bell with three short rings.

Scurlock, standing behind me, hesitated a moment and said something that I didn't understand, then jumped down to the crawl space beneath the cockpit. Seconds later frigid air rushed through the cockpit when he jettisoned the forward hatch. Over the roar of the engines I heard Scurlock's rebel yell as he dove out of the bomber. Woody, the bombardier, popped his head up between the pilots' seats and shouted, "Don't try to stay with her, Bill. Get out!"

I mouthed an okay and caught a glimpse of Woody pushing Joe, the navigator, out and then he followed him through the forward hatch.

Jim McGovern, the waist gunner, called, "We've got Lloyd out of the turret. We're leaving. See you, Lieutenant." Lloyd Thomas, the ball turret operator, was the one crew member I was most concerned about. He needed help getting out of the cramped quarters of the steel ball that hung from the belly of the bomber.

I reached up to hold my throat mike and acknowledge McGovern's call but was forced to grab the control column with both hands. It was impossible to keep the left wing up and I had to struggle to hold the bomber in a controlled spiral as it headed earthward. Apparently, the rudder or its control cables were damaged and my effort had little effect on stabilizing the bomber. The aileron and rudder trim tabs had no effect and I just couldn't compensate for the lost power from number two engine.

I watched the two German fighters that were following us down. They flew past on our port side and made a wide sweeping turn out ahead for a final frontal assault.

My parachute pack was down in the crawl space beneath the pilot's compartment. It was an English parachute and I wore just the harness. When the copilot, Louis Bianchi, got out of his seat, I shouted to him. "Hand me up my chute!"

Bianchi stepped down between the pilots' seats and grabbed my chest pack and handed it up to me. When I reached down with my left hand to grab it, the plane turned precipitously to the left in a steep vertical bank. I dropped the chute pack in my lap and again grabbed the yoke with both hands, trying to bring up the left wing.

For a few hectic seconds panic seized me. Could I get my chute on and get out of the burning plane? I forced the fear from my mind and tried to account for the crew. All the men in the front had left and McGovern confirmed that he, Gillet, Thomas, and Cobb were leaving by the rear cargo door. But I hadn't heard from Jim McBride, the tail gunner.

I called over the intercom, "Pilot to tail gunner. Bail out! Bail out! McBride, do you read?"

When I got no response after repeated calls, it suddenly dawned on me. *If McBride's gone, how the hell can he answer me?*

I struggled to clip the chest pack on while staring helplessly at the German fighters now well within firing range. In one last great effort, I pushed the right rudder down with both feet and with all my strength heaved the yoke back into my chest. The force I exerted on the controls pulled the Seventeen up sharply just as the two ME-109s were less than a few hundred yards away, speeding toward me on a collision course. The leader, who hadn't fired his canons — probably out of ammo — dove sharply to his right and barely avoided me. But his wing man, so intent on blasting me out of the sky, pulled up too late to his left and the fighter crashed into my raised right wing tip. The control column was ripped from my hands and the Seventeen shuttered from the impact. I regained control by shoving the yoke forward. A quick glance to my right caught sight of the ME-109 engulfed in flames. For a few fleeing seconds I watched mesmerized as the blazing German fighter rolled over and the pilot fell out and floated away.

While I fought desperately to keep the plane in a steep, controlled descending turn, I managed to get one hook of the chute pack clamped to the harness. I could only use my left hand and then only for a matter of seconds; I needed both hands and all my strength to keep the bomber from going into a spin. I just couldn't get the other clamp on my harness. On the verge of panic, I knew that my life depended on a strong, instinctive determination to live.

After several failed attempts, I decided to bail out with the one hook fastened to my chest harness. I released my seat belt, stripped away the oxygen mask and throat mike, reached over and held the pilot's control column down with my right hand, and got out of the copilot's seat. I stood for a moment between the seats with both hands on the control column in an attempt to force the left wing up. When that didn't work, I let go of the yoke, knowing I had to get out immediately before the bomber went completely out of control. I turned and bent down to go through the top turret as I'd planned to bail out through the open bomb bay. I instantly realized my mistake. The flames from the bomb bay seared my face viciously. It felt like I'd stuck my head in the open door of a blast furnace. The pain was excruciating and I quickly backed out, realizing this was not the way out. The smell of singed hair and burned skin was incidental to the desperate fear that raged through me. Confused and with no alternative, I retreated to the cockpit. I tried to stand but the forces on my body as the Seventeen headed earthward made it almost impossible. Grasping the backs of the pilots' seats, I tried to pull myself upright. The horizon had disappeared, in the wind screen, and instinctively

I grabbed the pilot's control column in an attempt to level the wings and pull up the nose. For some inherent reason it seemed important to me to get back in the pilot's seat and stop the plane's downward plunge. But the force of gravity held me down and I just couldn't get into the seat. Whether it was my effort in trying to stabilize the bomber or God's will, the Fortress seemed to hesitate just before rolling over. In those few precious seconds, I looked down between the seats and saw the open forward hatch. A voice within me shouted, "Get out! Get out now!" I let go of the control column, unknowingly clamped the other hook of the parachute pack to my chest harness, and dove for the opening. My shoulder hit the side of the hatch just as the bomber rolled over and I was thrown against the topside of the crawl space. I looked up and tried to raise my arms to the open hatch as the bomber headed downward in a vicious inverted dive. The turning plane pinned me helplessly upside down in the crawl space. As the Seventeen continued its slow roll, I managed to grab the sides of the open hatch and pulled myself up toward the opening. Exerting every bit of strength left in my body, I finally got my head and left shoulder out into the slip stream. The rush of air tore my helmet off and as I turned my head, I was momentarily blinded by an intense orange burst of fire followed immediately by a muffled explosion. I watched in stunned horror as the left wing was torn away from the fuselage. The plane's violent reaction to its lost wing hurled me out into space. My last thought, as I cleared the aircraft, was of Mary and an agonizing despair consumed me, knowing I would not be with her tonight.

I was suddenly overcome by a strange sensation of emptiness and apprehensive desolation as I fell through the cloudless, celestial solitude and away from the fiery bomber. The contrast between the weird sound of rushing air and the roar of the engines and the terror of the fire filled me with abandoned hope and yet a sense of relief. In a state of shock, I fell helplessly, not knowing or remembering how I managed to get out of the blazing bomber.

We had descended several thousand feet after our trouble started, but in my desperate flight from the pilot's compartment I failed to check the altimeter and had no idea how high I was above the ground. Determined to free-fall as far as possible and evade the enemy, I waited for what seemed to be an infinitely long time before pulling the rip cord. Abruptly, my chute popped open and jerked me upright.

It was a clear, magnificent day with unlimited visibility. Beneath me was a spectacular panoramic view of the German countryside. A large river, obviously the Rhine, was the most dominant feature, and my first thought was that the river would separate me from my crew. They would be on the near side while I would land on the other side, as they had left the plane before me.

I was much higher than I thought, possibly several thousand feet above the ground and realized I'd opened my parachute too soon. I saw seven or eight fires on the ground and my immediate assumption, after seeing so many bombers go down, was that they were burning American Fortresses.

I began to swing precariously in my parachute, I wondered whether it was properly fastened, and momentarily the fear of falling out of my harness consumed me. I looked up at the canopy and was tempted to pull on the shroud lines in an effort to stop the swaying and control my descent. But as I glanced around, the fear of falling out of my chute quickly faded with a far more frightening sight. Not more than a mile away was an Me 109 bearing down on me. I was overcome by the shocking realization: *after all this I'm going to be shot hanging helplessly in a parachute.* It had happened to some Allied airmen. The German pilot approached within a hundred yards of me, banked sharply, circled me once, and raised his arm in what could've been a friendly gesture or a salute and flew away. He may have been the lead German pilot on his way back to his base where he and his wing man, if he survived, would be credited with four kills for shooting down a four-engine aircraft.

A magnanimous feeling of relief flooded through me as my fear vanished and was replaced by a good measure of self-confidence. I looked to the ground and prepared to land, hoping to evade capture. I had prepared myself, as most airmen did, with a plan of what to do if forced to bail out. To this point, however, most of any planned actions had been ignored. My survival had been achieved through a strong instinct and determination to live. Approaching the ground, my thoughts were, *evade, I must get away, find someone to help me.* I knew that landing inside Germany made the prospect of evasion very remote but I had to try.

I landed in the backyard of a house in a small village. The minute my feet hit the ground, I pressed the release button on my chest pack and slipped out of the harness as the chute collapsed. A young boy suddenly appeared at the side of the house. He motioned to me and then turned and disappeared around the corner of the building. I immediately assumed that he wanted to help me and followed him around to the front of the house. And there, hurrying into the front yard, were two German soldiers dressed in uniforms of the Volksstrum with their rifles pointing directly at me. My thoughts of evading capture and getting back to England crumbled. One of the soldiers was an older man in his sixties, who was breathing heavily after he had apparently run some distance to get to me. The other was a young pimply faced teenager. They gestured toward me to get my hands up, which I did, and the old man said, "*Kommen* Sie."

I walked out ahead of them to the narrow road that led down to the village. At this point several people had gathered and followed me and the guards down the road. One person shouted something and then several others joined in. Although I couldn't understand them, they were obviously angry. Someone rapidly approached me from the rear and I felt two blows to my back and heard someone spit. I turned around to face my assailant, an older man, who immediately retreated. The old guard jabbed my chest with the butt of his rifle and impatiently motioned me forward. When I turned and started walking, I heard the bolt action of a rifle as one of the guards chamber a round. The other guard followed suit. *This is it*, I thought, looking up at the sky, silently praying and waiting, expecting any minute to feel the impact of bullets striking my back. But none came.

Recently an imbecilic American B-17 crew, calling themselves "Murder Inc", were shot down and captured, and the picture of the crew with that name blazoned on the backs of their leather jackets was seen in every newspaper in Germany. A fine example to support German propaganda that American airmen where a bunch of Chicago gangsters. Needless to say, my safety and welfare was at this point somewhat uncertain. My adversaries continued to crowd about me to the center of the village where another group of Germans met us. The guards directed me into a beer garden, where I stood surrounded by 20 or more people, most of whom were women. And they were angry.

One of the guards left and a woman pushed through the group. She came up to me and said, "Why do you come and bomb the German people? What have we done to America to make you bomb us?" She spoke excellent English. I looked at her and wanted to say, *What about Warsaw, Rotterdam, London, and Coventry?* but remained silent.

The harassment continued and the tension built. The picture in an English newspaper of an Royal Air Force (RAF) bomber crew hanging by their necks in the city square of Cologne flashed through my mind. The guard returned but stayed outside the circle of the group of civilians. The women crowded closer to me. The idea of striking a woman was repugnant, but if need be I was ready to defend myself by whatever means. Their jeers and shouts of anger intensified as they screamed and spit at me. Just as the circle of angry Germans tightened around me and they were on the verge of seizing me, a car stopped abruptly at the entrance to the beer garden. A German in a *Luftwaffe* uniform got out, and shouted and pushed his way through the crowd. The driver of the car joined him and they pulled me away from the angry group and shoved me into the car. I was driven back across the Rhine River to the local police station in the city of St. Goar. There they put me in a dungeonlike cell and gave me a sandwich of dark bread and sausage and a chipped, porcelain cup of water. No attempt was made to interrogate me. The guard slammed and locked the ancient, steel door and left me in a state of complete hopelessness.

For several minutes I stood there staring at the dismal, dark cell. Then I turned and sat on the edge of the iron cot. I placed my head in my hands as my despair and remorse reached a depth of misery I'd ever experienced. *God, what went wrong? Why did it have to happen? There must have been something I could've done to save the plane and get back to England! Why couldn't we get the fire out? If I had been flying from my normal position in the left seat, would I've caught the fire sooner and been able to put it out? Had all of my crew survived? They were so close to finishing and so eager to go home. Why this time? It was my fault. I'd let down the crew and, most of all, Mary.* Self-accusations and incriminating thoughts flooded though my mind. The mission was a disaster from the start. But as screwed up as it was, I still should have made it back to England and Mary as I had on my previous sorties.

* * * *

The twin missions to Schweinfurt and Regensburg on 17 August 1943 were flown by the largest bomber force ever assembled by the Eighth Air Force. Three hundred seventy-six B-17s, "Flying Fortresses," in twenty-one groups were scheduled to make their deepest, unescorted penetration into Germany. It was inconceivable to think that there were just four operational bombardment groups when my tour started in April of 1943. And during that four-month period more than two hundred bombers and their crews were lost in air battles over Europe.

The target of the First Air Division, the main bomber force, was the ball-bearing works at Schweinfurt; the remaining aircraft with the Third Air Division would strike the Messerschmitt factory in Regensburg. The latter force was scheduled to leave fifteen minutes before the main bomber formation, bomb Regensburg, then shuttle to bases in North Africa and not return directly to the United Kingdom.

The mission from the start was a complete foul-up caused by bad weather over England, poor judgment, and faulty decisions made by the Eighth Air Force Bomber Command. A five-hour delay started the disaster. Instead of a fifteen-minute separation there was a three-and-a-half hour gap between the two departing air divisions. During that time, the *Luftwaffe* had gathered the greatest fighter force ever assembled to attack what they thought would be the returning Third Air Division. (They rose meeting the incoming groups of the First Air Division instead as they entered German airspace on their way to Schweinfurt.) The air battle started over Belgium the moment the Allied escort fighters left the bomber formation. The American Fortresses were under constant attack by hundreds of German fighters all the way to the target.

I was leading the low flight in the high composite group, part of the 101st Wing which was leading the bomber force to Schweinfurt. I was flying the aircraft from the right seat for better vision of the group leader in the flight slightly above, forward and to my right. Lieutenant Jim Lockhart, leading my second element, had left us shortly after the formation reached the German border. Lockhart's two wing men had aborted and he apparently decided to fill one of the vacated slots in the 91st Bomb Group beneath us. Our three-ship element continued on with my two wing men, Lieutenants Peek and Wieneth.

On the third fierce frontal attack by the *Luftwaffe*, Wieneth's bomber, flying on my left wing, was hit hard. The Fortress was literally blown apart, tearing the right wing away from the fuselage. No parachutes were seen leaving the flaming B-17 as it fell to earth.

We survived one more attack but not the next. A German 20 mm round ripped through our aircraft and set number two engine on fire. After several attempts to extinguish the fire failed we were forced to abandon our aircraft.

* * * *

Sitting in my desolate cell, it suddenly dawned on me that it had been sixteen hours since my last meal. I was hungry but just couldn't stomach more than a few bites of the unpalatable sandwich. I finally fell into a disturbed sleep after much soul-searching and thoughts of Mary. Most agonizing was the realization that I would not be with her tonight as we had planned, and probably not for many more nights to come.

I was awakened during the night by rats scrambling across my body to get to the unfinished sandwich. The scary incident was no doubt a wretched preview of the desperate times that I faced.

Chapter 2

Captured

In the morning the guards took me from my cell and back across the Rhine River to the St. Goar railroad station. And there, to my amazement, standing on the platform surrounded by guards were Denver Woodward, Joe Newberry, Lloyd Thomas, Jim McGovern, and Ray Gillet. My initial reaction, although I was grateful and relieved to see them, was somewhat subdued by the guilt I felt for putting them in this most desperate situation. But they, ignoring their guards, rushed forward and greeted me warmly and enthusiastically.

Woody grabbed and vigorously shook my hand. "Thank God, you made it, Bill."

Joe shook my hand and gave me a broad smile, followed by Lloyd, Jim, and Ray. It was a very emotional and unsettling meeting. Each one seemed relieved and truly glad to see me. Their reception helped immensely to reconcile the reprehensible guilt I felt.

"What about the other guys? How about McBride? Did he get out?" I asked anxiously.

"Yes sir, I saw his chute open. Lloyd and I were last to leave the rear and we all got out," Gillet offered fervently.

"Well, I really feel like hell letting you guys down. Damn, we should've been able to put out that bloody fire."

"Look, Bill, we all got out and we're all alive. And that, thank God, is more than we could possibly hope for," replied Joe. It was a very unusual and emotional response from our normally passive navigator.

Our happy and grateful reunion was disrupted by the noisy arrival of the train that emersed us in a cloud of steam and soot. We were put into a third-class compartment. The accommodations were slightly better than a boxcar, which would later become very familiar to most prisoners of war.

We were in Germany near the Rhine River, that was obvious, but weren't exactly sure where. "Where do you think we are, Joe?" I asked.

"We should be about fifty miles northwest of Frankfurt. We were quite a bit south of our course when we bailed out. Afraid I didn't much notice where we were when the fire got out of control and you told us to get out."

"Me neither, Joe. The only thing I remember was seeing the Rhine River. I landed on the other side and they brought me over. I figured the river would separate me from you guys."

The guards didn't seem to mind our talking. And when Woody made several deliberate statements about escaping, they appeared unconcerned. We weren't sure whether they understood English, but I noticed one guard tighten the grip on his machine pistol and put his finger on the trigger guard.

We peered anxiously at the German countryside as the train followed the Rhine River southward. Looking closely, I noticed that some of the train stations still had the name of the town or village posted and we tried to speculate where we were. Woody got no reaction when he asked the guards where we were headed.

After a long two-hour ride with many stops, the train pulled into a large steel-and-glass enclosure, obviously a major passenger rail terminal. Joe asked the guard if it was Frankfurt. He got a slight nod in response. On the platform we met a group of guarded American airmen. I didn't recognize anyone, but they seemed glad to see us. They confirmed that it was Frankfurt and said they were being taken to a temporary POW camp for interrogation.

We were all loaded into a couple of trucks and taken a short distance to a camp called Dulag Luft. There the officers were separated from the enlisted men and each group was put into a small barbed-wire enclosure. Joe, Woody, and I joined about twenty other crew members among whom was Louis Bianchi.

When my copilot saw me, his face lit up and he broke out in a big, happy grin. He ran over and grabbing me said, "Boy, Bill, am I glad to see you. Damn, I was really worried about you getting out of the plane." He turned to Woody and Joe and hugged them as well.

I was surprised by his enthusiasm, as Louis was not one to show a lot of emotion. There were some familiar faces among the other POWs, but no one that I knew by name. Perhaps that was why Bianchi was so glad to see us. Fear and despair, apparently, are not too hard to accept when you are among friends.

I became angry and resentful when we were herded into pens like cattle. The loss of freedom can have a very degrading effect on a person. After the initial show of cheerfulness at being together, everyone soon became solemn and quiet. Several hours later we were moved out of the barbed-wire enclosure and into a building. An English-speaking guard took down our names, ranks, and serial numbers.

The first two days and nights were spent in what the prisoners called the Snake Pit. It was apparently a holding area, approximately fifteen by thirty feet, that reminded me of an indoor handball court with wooden walls and floor and a high ceiling. There were no chairs, tables, or bunks. About ninety to one hundred of us were crowded into the space with just enough room to stand, or sit with your knees pulled up to your chest. The food consisted of two pieces of black bread, a bowl of watery barley gruel, and weak lukewarm tea.

The most difficult part of early confinement was the mental anguish one suffered, not so much the physical discomfort. It was impossible to clear one's mind of the despair and gloom of being imprisoned. My thoughts kept returning to the missions we had flown and how wonderful it was to see that coast of England after a rough raid. And after landing, how I would rush to my quarters, bathe and dress, and head for London and Mary. Most of all I missed her and could not reconcile the fact that I might not see her again.

The interned men rarely spoke, and if they did it was in anger or to curse the Germans for causing their predicament. Everyone appeared to be out of cigarettes which only added to their ill temper and aggravation. Most seemed satisfied to remain silent and content to keep their gloomy thoughts to themselves. No one seemed to know how long we would be held like animals in a pen. At intervals a German guard would appear, call the names of four prisoners, and take them out. My crew and I were finally escorted out after forty-four hours in the pit. From there we were taken to individual cells. The prisonlike room would later be known as the cooler. The cell was about eight feet long and six feet wide, clean but with a strong smell of disinfectant. The only furnishings in the room were an iron cot, a wooden stool, and a slop bucket. The bed was covered with a dark blue blanket over a mattress filled with wood shavings resting on seven wooden slats. There was a small window about seven feet up from the floor that was painted over. The only illumination in the cell was from a light bulb hanging from the ceiling that was turned on and off from the outside at odd times. The pleasure and relief of having more space soon gave way to a feeling of loneliness and abandoned hope.

I felt completely isolated, even though I knew there were other POWs in similar cells. I saw them when I entered mine. The walls must be exceptionally thick because when I called out there was no response.

Four days of solitude and mental incrimination with nothing to do but think. Again the same questions plagued my thoughts. *Why this time? We had come so close. What went wrong?* I just couldn't stop the feeling of self-condemnation. It was my fault and I should have been able and capable of getting my crew back. And most of all back to Mary. God, how I missed her.

* * * *

I had met Mary Chapman on my first night in London. I was with three friends, former flying school classmates. We met and journeyed to London on 10 April, a Saturday. After dinner, my friend, Norman Retchin, introduced me to the Astor, a private bottle club in the London's West End. Norm had arrived in the U.K. three weeks before I had and was assigned to the 91st Bomb Group at Bassingbourn, where later, I would also be stationed. He had been to London several times and seemed to know his way around. Having just arrived in England, I was assigned to the Combat Replacement Crew Center at Bovington, a base a short distance from London. It was an induction center to prepare the new crews for combat and above all how to comport themselves and respect the English people.

Being an American, it was a simple matter to become an instant member of the club. Shortly after we were seated, I was attracted by a dark haired, beautiful young woman sitting with an older couple across the dance floor. I became fascinated by her animated gestures and expression in a cheerful discussion with her companions. She was incredibly attractive and had the most unusual and magnificent eyes I'd ever seen. When my friends noticed my acute interest in the girl, they suggested that I go over and introduce myself, which I finally did after some very forceful persuasion on their part. Up close, she was even more beautiful and I awkwardly stumbled through an invitation to dance, which she accepted. Her closeness while dancing had me trembling with sensuous thoughts and I just couldn't think of something to say. She finally broke the silence by asking me how long I'd been in England. I told her three days and then stupidly added, "Now that we, the Americans, are here, we'll take care of the Germans." That was as far as I got. Eyes flashing with anger, she pushed away from me and responded vehemently, "We've done very well without you. Why don't you go back where you came from, Yank!" It was unlike me to boast and I wondered why I'd made such an overbearing remark. I was ashamed and apologized profusely, realizing that my foolish remark could end any hope of a relationship I might have with this beautiful creature.

Through the course of the evening, however, she forgave me, and my spirits, along with my desire, soared. When her friends and my buddies left us alone, we stayed and talked until the club closed. A short time later I found myself walking down Piccadilly Road in the middle of the night with the most bewitchingly beautiful girl I'd ever met. We were caught in my first air raid when an antiaircraft battery suddenly started firing not forty feet away as we were casually strolling beside Green Park. I was amazed at her indifference to the raid while I was noticeably shaken. After the all clear, we found a taxi. Immediately after settling in the back seat we were in each other's arms as though we'd been waiting all evening for this moment, both with the same intense desire to devour each other with deep, breathless kisses. Our passionate embrace ended when the taxi stopped at her apartment block and I was forced to release her from my arms. After a warm embrace and a more subdued kiss at her door, she gently pushed me away and asked me to call her in the morning. When I returned to the taxi, I sat there for several minutes trembling with excitement over our passionate coupling. Never before had I ever experienced such a sensual arousal and passion that this girl elicited in me.

We met the following day, Sunday, and spent a wonderful afternoon together walking through Hyde Park and stopping later for tea in a cozy little cafe. A new experience for me but I thoroughly enjoyed it. We did little more than hold hands and talk. But just being with this fascinating and vivacious young woman was the most exciting and pleasant time I'd ever experienced. The day ended at Euston rail station where we kissed goodbye in an awkward but promising embrace.

During the following week at Bovington, reality set in and my conscience took over. I had been seriously involved with a woman in America for more than two years. Clare Beatty was a wealthy heiress who had been separated from her husband when we first became involved. He had later died and now that she was finally free, I had felt obligated to ask her to marry me before being sent overseas. She considered it best to wait until I returned, but I felt committed. The infatuation and the desire I felt for Mary Chapman was far beyond any feeling I ever had for Clare. I realized it would be very easy to become seriously involved and fall in love with Mary, the most beautiful and fascinating girl I had ever met, and that would be wrong.

* * * *

Solitary confinement. I heard about it. Saw men enduring it in the movies and read about it, but nothing, absolutely nothing could prepare a person for the despair and loneliness of being locked up by oneself. I tried to exercise by walking four short steps forward and back. But that soon became monotonous and I gave up. I tried push-ups. But the slim diet of a bowl of thin soup, water, and a slice of black bread each day left me with little energy or enthusiasm to continue. So I spent most of my time lying on my cot, staring up at the ceiling and thinking. They had taken away my freedom, but damn it, they can't stop my thought process, and most important my mental ability to think. I thought about my mother, *How sad and worried she would be after receiving that dreaded message from the War Department: "We regret to inform you that your son is missing in action. . ." God, how awful for Mom! And Dad, he too. If I could just tell them that I'm okay and not to worry.*

I thought about how much I wanted to get to England and help the people in their struggle against Hitler, and how upset my parents were when I left my job in July 1940 and went to Canada to enlist in the Royal Canadian Air Force (RCAF). There were more volunteers there than they could accommodate and I was told to wait until they called me. I went back to my home in Scarsdale, New York, and waited. And waited, and after three months, I gave up and enlisted in the US Army Air Corps. It wasn't until our group was ready to take off for overseas in March that I heard what really happened to my Canadian venture. I received a letter from my father who shamefully admitted that he and my mother decided to withhold a letter from the RCAF that arrived a few days after I returned from Canada. It was a letter for me to report for duty in the RCAF. They had opened it and decided not to show it to me. They just wanted to keep me out of harm's way and didn't want me involved in a foreign war where I would have to forfeit my citizenship. I was angry and disturbed but as I was leaving for England as a B-17 aircraft commander, I forgave them. Now my parents are faced with all the fears and anxieties that they tried so desperately to avoid. I wondered, *How long will it take for them to know that I'm alive?*

On the sixth day a guard appeared at my cell and motioned for me to follow him. I was taken to a large room where a young *Luftwaffe* lieutenant sat behind a desk. When the guard left and closed the door, the German looked up and said, "Ah, *Herr* Wheeler, I am *Leutnant* Schmieter. Please sit down." He pointed to a chair beside the desk. The lieutenant was rather small of stature but immaculately dressed in a well, tailored uniform. His English was perfect and precise. He picked up a silver cigarette case from the desk, opened and held it out to me, and said, "Cigarette, *bitte*."

I responded almost too quickly, "No thanks," without thinking and was then sorry for refusing. A smoke was something I desperately wanted.

When the German said, "Are you sure you won't have one?" I refused again, thinking that since I hadn't had a cigarette for more than a week, it was probably a good time to quit.

The German lieutenant then said, "Ahh no matter, but if you change your mind, help yourself." He left the case open in front of me. He picked up a prepared form and said, "First, we must fill out this form for the Red Cross so they can notify your family that you are a prisoner of war." He picked up a pen and said, "Now. Your given name is William and you are a first lieutenant. What is your serial number, *bitte?*"

I replied, "AO791528."

"What was the designation of your squadron and bomb group?" he asked very casually.

"I am only required to give you my name, rank, and serial number."

He smiled saying, "Yes, but I must complete this form for the Red Cross." He held up the form. "As you can see, it is addressed to the International Red Cross. And it must be filled out so they can notify your family."

"I am not required to give you any additional information."

He said, "But you must."

I shook my head slightly and remained silent.

Schmieter looked displeased and impatient and said sharply, "I must insist that you give me this information." I remained silent and held eye contact with the German until he looked down and removed a file from his desk drawer. He opened the file and said, "This is very foolish of you to be so uncooperative. Because I have all the information I need in this file. And now I will have to do this for you so your family will not worry about you." He reached over, extracted a cigarette from the case, made a gesture to me, and again I shook my head negatively.

He then added, "You know, I have traveled all over the United States. I can tell what part of the country an American comes from, just by listening to him speak. I'm sure not many of your fellow officers can do that. It requires a great deal of skill and intelligence, wouldn't you agree?" He hesitated, waiting, and when I didn't reply he continued, "You do not have a New York accent. Why?"

I stared back at him, hoping that my expression didn't reveal the surprise I felt, but said nothing.

"Now," he said, "let's get on with the job at hand. If you refuse to help me, I must fill this form out for you. Let me see. You were a member of the 401st Bomb Squadron, stationed at Bassingbourn in the 91st Bomb Group. You have flown how many terror raids against us, twenty-three or twenty-four? You were very fortunate to get back from that sortie to Gelsenkirchen last Thursday. I must say, it was not a very well, organized mission and a very poor performance by the Eighth Air Force. You lost over thirty aircraft."

I attempted to look unimpressed but was sure I failed to hide my astonishment at the information the Germans had. *Leutnant* Schmieter went on at some length to tell me how much he knew about me and my organization. At one point he got up, walked to one wall, and drew a curtain aside. There almost identical to the briefing at Bassingbourn was the large map of Europe, showing the Fortress formations, their departure bases, assembly points, and the routes to Schweinfurt and Regensburg. There were also numerous red crosses on the map, apparently where our bombers had been shot down. I tried to locate my downed Seventeen.

The German lieutenant continued to flaunt his knowledge about me and the American air force. Then, very indifferently, he said, "It says that you enlisted in the US Army Air Corps in December 1940. And you were commissioned in July 1942 when you received your pilot rating. When did you leave enlisted status?" I was almost caught up by his casual tone and just stopped myself from answering him. I looked at the German and smiled, shaking my head.

At this point the interrogator became quite annoyed and said, "*Leutnant* Wheeler, I have been very patient with you and helpful, so that your mother will learn that you are now safe in German hands. But if you will not cooperate, perhaps another week in the cooler may make you more responsive." He pressed a buzzer and a guard appeared who led me back to my cell.

It was incredible that the Germans had so much information about me. Did they have a file on every American pilot? It was hard to believe. Apparently they just wanted to know what might be considered a very insignificant date, when and where my pilot training started. Lying back on my bunk, I thought about the lectures we sat through at Bovington, the Combat Crew Replacement Center, and realized what the Germans were doing. They were a very meticulous race and needed that little bit of information to complete a very comprehensive file on me. But immediately another thought came to mind, *Once you think, "Hell, they know everything about me . . . what difference does it make how much I tell them." They've got you.*

They get that little something from you, that insignificant date, and then you're on a slippery slope and may reveal more important information, because what the hell, they already know everything. So I resolved to give them nothing.

The solitude and misery of the worst kind continued with nothing to do but lie on my cot. I wondered, *How long can I endure this? Should I tell them the seemingly insignificant bit of information they wanted? Is it worth it to lie here alone in the damnable silence of this bloody cell.*

I thought about how eager I had been to get to England. It had been an obsession with me. And when I finally made it, those few months were the best of my life. I just wanted to stay in England and continue flying until the end of the war. I had finally reached my goal, I was a pilot and fighting against Hitler's Germany. I wanted all the glory and responsibility that went with being an aircraft commander. My life, I felt, had been a waste until the time I received my appointment to flight school. It all started that magnificent day when I soloed at Carlstrom Field in Florida. I remember it so clearly. One of the first in my class to solo and what a glorious day it was. Alone in the open cockpit of a Stearman. Shortly after take-off, I let go of the stick and threw both hands up into the slip stream and shouted with sheer joy. I looked down at the earth beneath me and realized that I was up there alone and for the first time I truly felt the real sensation of flying. Suddenly, the plane lurched to the left. In my excitement, I must have kicked the left rudder causing the biplane to slip off in a diving turn. I quickly grabbed the stick, pushed the nose down, and got on the right rudder pedal. I managed to bring the Stearman under control about two hundred feet above the ground. It scared the living hell out of me and I realized flying could be great fun but it could also be deadly dangerous.

Now, here locked in a German cell, my flying days were over, at least for a long, long time. I'll never forget that wonderful, exuberant feeling of being so alive and exhilarated when letting down over the coast of England after returning from a mission to German. Would I ever feel like that again?

After six more wretched days, I was taken back to visit the sharp little German lieutenant and after a few polite pleasantries, he inevitably got around to asking me the same question, and each time he got a negative response from me. So it was back to the cooler.

Three days later, I was again ushered into Schmieter's office and when I again refused to answer his questions, his attitude changed and he became angry and overbearing and I was sent back to the cooler. However, I was released the following day. I later learned that my stay in the cooler might have been longer, had it not been for the great influx of prisoners from the Schweinfurt and Regensburg missions. There was not adequate space to hold and methodically process and interrogate the American airmen as the Germans had done in the past.

Along with fifteen other fellow officers, we were assembled and led down to a large barbed-wire enclosure, the POW compound. As we approached the barrier at the main gate, we heard men shouting and cheering. On the other side of the fence a large crowd of Americans and Englishmen gathered. They waved and shouted at us, calling out to individuals in our group by name. I heard someone shout, "Hey, Wheeler, they finally got you! Welcome to your new *Kriegie* home." I didn't recognize the voice but saw many familiar faces, among them Joe, Woody, and Louis.

The two gates at the main entrance to the compound were separated by a distance of about twenty feet to create a small holding area. We were led through one gate and waited while it was locked before the other was opened. When the inner gate was opened, we were moved into the compound and were swarmed by fellow POWs. We were welcomed by loud cheerful greetings and raucous remarks, along with much handshaking, hugging, and backslapping. Laughter and smiling faces surrounded us. Cigarettes and candy bars were forced on us. What a wonderful feeling it was to be among friends and comrades again.

An RAF officer finally settled the group down and addressed us: "Welcome to Dulag Luft. I am Squadron Leader Hawkins." He paused as we acknowledged his introduction, smiled, and continued: "I must say I am not exactly overwhelmed with joy meeting you here and under such bloody circumstances, but so be it, we'll try to make your stay here as comfortable as possible. First order of the day, however, will be to get you fed. Your quarters, a bit of an exaggeration to say the least, have been arranged. We have tried to get you together with your crew or friends. Now, if you will follow me to the mess hall, we'll see to your most urgent need—food."

After sixteen days of isolation, gloom, despair, bread and water, the greeting received by my fellow airmen was most welcome and pleasant. I found it difficult to believe that under such circumstances one could actually feel pleased and cheerful. It amazed me how quickly all the despondency and dismay I'd suffered over the past two weeks suddenly vanished.

My spirits soared and a big smile spread across my face when Woody told me, "Wait until you see the chow they serve here. Five meals a day. These Brits sure know how to live."

Then Louis said, "We've saved a bottom bunk for you, Bill. And we're all together. It isn't too bad here except for the damn barbed wire."

Joe followed up with, "This is just a temporary camp. The British run it. We'll probably be moved in a few days to a permanent camp." He hesitated, then added, "How about that German interrogator? What a slick little artist he was. He greeted us with 'For you the war is over, so settle back, cooperate, and enjoy our hospitality.' What a dreamer."

Recalling the information the German officer had shown me, I said, "He certainly surprised me with the amount of information he had on us. He apparently wanted something from me. Something quite insignificant. After three attempts, I guess he gave up. But I can see how they can sweat it out of a person after several weeks of solitary confinement. It's hell. Guess I was lucky to get out as soon as I did."

"Well, we were in there for five days and then they had to move us to make room for all the new prisoners. You know, we lost sixty Seventeens on that Schweinfurt raid," Joe went on to say. "The British here give the latest war news to us. It's called 'Gen.' They smuggled radio receivers into camp and listen to the BBC broadcast every night, type it up, and read it in each hut every day before lockup. They sure have things well organized. It helps to know how the war is going. We're only allowed the German news and if they found the hidden radio they'd confiscate it."

"How about Wieneth and his crew? Are they here? I recognized a few other guys here from our group."

"No, I haven't seen him or his crew, and I checked to see if any of them are in the camp hospital. No luck. God, I hope they got out of that plane! But from what Lloyd said and he watched it go down from the ball turret, it looked like no one got out. He saw no chutes," replied Woody.

That horrible picture of Wieneth's Seventeen, flying on my right wing, being blown out of the sky and going down wingless in flames flashed through my mind. I did not respond immediately, silently trying to dismiss the terrible scene. Wieneth had flown his first mission with me on 21 May to Whelmshaven. A 20 mm round tore through the cockpit and Wieneth's face was cut badly by the glass and metal from the shattered instrument panel in front of him. They stitched him up in the hospital and he was back flying with me to Bremen on 13 June at which time I checked him out as a combat-ready aircraft commander. On the Schweinfurt mission he was piloting Lieutenant Steven Cook's crew who had just arrived from the States and was required to fly his first mission with an experienced pilot.

I later learned that Cook was the only survivor. He was literally blown out of the bomber, and when he regained consciousness he managed to open his chute and land uninjured. Cook evaded that night and the following morning while walking along an isolated country road he saw a motorcycle approaching him. There were open fields on both sides of the road and no place to hide. The vehicle stopped several yards ahead of him and when a German officer stepped out of the sidecar, Cook raised his hands to surrender. The German officer walked up to him, withdrew his Luger, and shot Cook in the stomach. He fell in the drainage ditch and the Germans drove away. A short time later a farmer found Cook and took him to a German hospital. The wound had closed so the doctor did not remove the bullet. Cook remained in the hospital for several weeks and one day he felt a small protrusion in the center of his back. He asked the doctor to look at it. He did and simply plucked the lead slug out of the American's back and gave it to him. Just before Cook was being sent to the Stalag at Barth a German officer demanded that Cook give him the slug that was removed from his back. Cook refused and was told if he did not give him the bullet, Cook's friend, a Polish prisoner working in the hospital, would be shot. He reluctantly relinquished the bullet to the German.

After clearing my thoughts of the tragic ending of Wieneth and Cook's crew, I said, "This is a hell of a lot better than the cooler and that damn snake pit, but I sure don't like the idea of spending the rest of the war here. Have you heard anything about the possibility of escaping? Do they have anything organized?"

Joe replied, "Yeah, they have a group called the 'X' committee who controls all the escape activity. I don't think anyone has gotten out of this camp. Besides, the Brits have it pretty well sewn up. You'd have to be here awhile before you can get into the organization. Probably have to wait until we get to our permanent camp. And from what I hear, it's further east and deeper into Germany."

When we reached the mess hall, Louis said, "We're in Hut 17, Bill. We'll see you down there when you finish chow, okay?"

"You bet. And it's great seeing you guys again. I'm glad we're going to be together. See you in awhile." They left, and the sixteen new POWs followed the RAF officer into a large wooden hut, where we were seated. There were about twenty long wooden tables that seated ten or twelve on wood benches. When we were settled, two RAF enlisted men put a big bowl of boiled potatoes and a huge pile of Spam and corned beef on each table. After that was passed around, they brought out pitchers of hot tea, biscuits, and jam. I was very hungry. The man next to me passed me a bowl of potatoes, and a platter of meat followed. I was never very fond of Spam or corned beef, but boy, did it taste good.

The RAF officer told us that this was in fact a temporary camp and we would be moved to a permanent camp for air force officers, probably to Stalag Luft III at Sagan, a small town near Frankfurt on the Oder, about sixty miles southeast of Berlin. We were also told that each hut here had a leader or person in charge, usually the ranking man in the hut, who would brief us all on *Kriegie* life and what was expected of us while we were at Dulag. If they missed anything, our comrades would undoubtedly fill us in.

One large plate of food was as much as I needed and I turned down a second helping, knowing that it would probably give me a hell of a bellyache. Not so with some of the other prisoners; they stuffed themselves until they could hardly stand.

We were told where to pick up a palliasse, blankets, and toilet kit, the latter being a gift from the YMCA. We were also informed that each prisoner was entitled to one Red Cross food parcel a week, either English, Canadian, or American. "That's in addition to the German ration, which is only about 1200 calories a day, mainly potatoes, bread and jam with meat perhaps, once a week." The RAF officer said: "Their ersatz coffee is not much more than ground-up pine bark, but the sugar is okay. Because of the transient nature of this camp, we have consolidated the staples in the parcels with the German rations and prepare the food here for all the men. However, each of you will be given the cigarettes, chocolate, and other goodies from your parcels. Take care of the clothes you're wearing because clothing supplies here are very scarce." He went on to say, "You'll get some underwear and socks here and the rest will be furnished at the Stalag. But if you desperately need something to wear, we'll get it for you." The Germans took most of the flying gear the Americans were wearing when they were captured. They took my flight suit and sheepskin-lined boots. My sole possessions were a leather jacket, turtleneck sweater, and pink uniform trousers. I was wearing loafers under my boots and figured I'd have to do something about getting a more durable pair of shoes.

Louis was waiting outside when we left the mess hut. "I'll give you a hand with your mattress and gear, Bill."

"Thanks, Louis. Boy, that food sure tasted good. You know, as bad as it is being a prisoner, locked up like we are, it's not that bad when you're with friends, and all the guys who are in the same bloody mess. I don't think I've every felt so damn miserable and depressed as I did alone in that god awful cell the first night after being captured. It's not too bad here, but I don't know how anyone can stand being confined, locked up like an animal. You must develop a herd mentality. You don't realize how great freedom is until you lose it. But seeing and being with you guys again have made me feel a hell of a lot better."

"I know how you feel, Bill. It's rough. But we're alive and I guess that's something to be thankful for. Right?"

"You can say that again." I picked up my palliasse, a coarse white linen mattress cover, open at one side with tie strings. Louis showed me how much wood shavings and straw to put in it and how to fashion a pillow at one end. Bianchi threw it over his shoulder and said he would take it to their hut. I picked up my ration of cigarettes, chocolate, clothing, and a shaving kit. The British airmen at the supply hut gladly traded my loafers for a pair of slightly used black RAF high-top shoes. I'd later be very grateful for the exchange.

I found Hut 17 in the middle of the compound. It was divided into eight large rooms, each one about two hundred feet square with two smaller rooms at either end. The large rooms had six double-decker bunks and six double wooden lockers. A wooden table, eight feet long, and two benches completed the furnishing.

Woody and Joe were in our assigned combine and I was pleasantly surprised to see Gary Wilson, a classmate of mine, lying in his bunk reading. He stood and greeted me warmly. The last time I had seen Wilson was on 12 August, just after bomb release when his Seventeen collided with Lieutenant Fred Arp's B-17 on the mission to Gelsenkirchen.

Gary said, "Joe and Woody told me how you managed to get back after you left us over the target. You looked like you were in serious trouble. Arp and I got tangled up just after that. We were damn lucky. Fortunately, we got our crew out. Arp and his crew are here with us. They're in the compound with the guys in my crew."

"Well, I'm sure glad you both made it," I said. "I felt like hell leaving you but we just couldn't keep up with the formation. Number four was hit by flak just as we turned over the IP and the damn prop wouldn't feather. I had to drop down to the deck. It was a real rough flight and we were damn lucky to get back." There was a brief silence, I guess we were all thinking about that harrowing flight back to England on the deck."

Then Joe said, "Let's go, it's tea time."

"No, thanks, I just ate more than I have in two weeks." I folded the blanket over my cot and put the few personal possessions in my assigned locker. I said, "I'd like to get settled down and look around a bit. See what this place is like." As my crew and Wilson left, a feeling of gloom and loneliness settled over me and I decided to get outside. It was a sunny warm day in early September. I thought about what Bianchi said: "We're alive," and that should certainly be some comfort to me. So I did feel somewhat better. But I thought, *I have to keep thinking about an escape and to get back to England. Back to Mary.*

I walked down between the huts, spaced about thirty feet apart, counting eighteen of them. One of the huts had a little vegetable garden and a small patch of grass. In front of it, two RAF types were sunning themselves in chairs built out of packing cases. They apparently were part of the camp's permanent party. The rest of the huts were quite bare, surrounded by brown sandy soil. A soccer—or football, as the British call it—game was in progress on a large area in the center of the camp. I watched the game for awhile, admiring the skill of the Englishmen and other nationalities playing the game. Most of them were very adept at using their heads as well as their feet. The expressions from the spectators amused me with such sayings as "bloody lovely," "by jove, good go," and "jolly good show, old boy."

When the game broke up, I wandered to the perimeter of the camp, where dozens of POWs were walking. Internment has a way of drawing captives toward the fence that confines them. It's a place to walk and think about freedom and your loved ones. Looking out much like caged animals moving back and forth behind bars. The prisoners walked beside a low barrier made of a two-inch strip of wood about two feet high that circled the compound. Twenty feet beyond that barrier was the barbed-wire fence consisting of two fences, ten feet apart and about twelve feet high. Between them was coiled barbed wire or concertina four feet high. The elevated guard towers were about twenty-five feet high and three hundred feet apart, each with a guard standing behind a mounted machine gun between two searchlights. The area between the low wooden barrier and the fence was called no man's land." If a prisoner stepped into it without permission from the guard, he could be shot.

I joined a fellow *Kriegie* walking the perimeter. His name was Frank Carey, a pilot from the 381st Bomb Group, who was shot down, like me, on the Schweinfurt mission. I probably saw him go down that dreadful day. He was flying in the low group in the lead wing and at their altitude they took a hell of a beating. Carey got out of the cooler three days ago and gave me a good briefing on the dos and don'ts of being a prisoner. "The guard towers are called 'Goon Boxes'," he said, "and guards in the grey overalls with the metal rods are ferrets. They spend their time looking for any indications of escape activity like signs of a tunnel or overhearing someone talking about getting out.

"We'll all be leaving in a couple of days to a permanent camp. This place is getting overcrowded. And I don't think the Brits like the idea of having too many Yanks around. They've got a nice little deal here and I think they want to keep it that way."

I later rejoined my crew in their hut just in time to accompany them to the evening meal. Woody made a very appropriate observation, "Don't knock it, Bill. This is the only time of day I find this lousy place halfway bearable. And what's more, they have an evening snack just before lock up. Five meals a day. Not bad, these Brits. They certainly know how to make the best of a bad situation."

Joe added, "You know, there are a lot of guys here that are completely satisfied that they don't have to fly and get shot at anymore. For them, the war is over, and as long as they get enough to eat, they're going to lie back in their sacks and wait it out. If not here, at a much better permanent camp. And according to the Germans, Stalag Luft III is a real country club with a swimming pool and everything."

"Well not me," I proclaimed. "I'm going to get out of this place one way or the other. I'll be damned if I spend the rest of the war here."

Chapter 3

German Transport

Two days later, one hundred and sixty American air force officers were given Red Cross parcels to be shared between two men and marched out of the camp to a rail siding. We were lined up in front of four boxcars of the famous World War I vintage—40 *hommes* or 8 *chevaux*. The German guards counted forty men and then ordered each group to get into their assigned boxcar. As a deterrent to escaping, we were ordered to remove our shoes. The guards methodically gathered, tagged, and stowed them in the baggage car.

I pulled myself up to get in the car and immediately turned around and jumped down, shouting, "No way."

The few other POWs that climbed into the car with me did the same. The German guards started shouting and pointed their machine pistols menacingly at us. The car was filthy and stunk; it smelled like a sheep pen. A sleazy little German major appeared and began screaming at an American colonel, motioning for him to get aboard. An English-speaking German guard appeared shortly and explained to the American colonel that there was nothing he could do. The guard said with some hesitance that we must get on board the freight train because it had to leave in thirty minutes and if we refused, it was possible that some of the prisoners would be shot. The colonel offered to sweep out the cars and argued vehemently with the

German major, but the bastard just stood there looking away. The colonel finally turned his back on the German and said to the officers grouped around him, "It looks like we'll have to ride in these filthy, stinking boxcars. So let's get on and get it over with."

The only accommodations were several boards stretched across the car that served as benches. The floor was covered with a couple of inches of black soot and sheep dung. The last American to board was a stocky lieutenant colonel. Two POWs helped him up. His shirt was open and he had a large wound in his upper left chest. He had just been released from a German hospital and although the wound was bandaged, it was still open and draining. They got him settled near the door. I thought, *If he can take this lousy accommodation in his condition we certainly can.* I later learned that the wounded airman was Melvin McNickle, who had an identical twin named Marvin. Both were lieutenant colonels and had been inseparable since graduating from West Point. The twins were commanders of separate P-47 squadrons in the same fighter group stationed in England. Melvin, flying a P-47 while escorting a bomber formation, had taken a 20-mm hit in the cockpit. His canopy jammed and he couldn't bail out. He passed out as his fighter headed for the ground and woke up two days later in a German hospital. He was told that two German farmers found him unconscious and pulled him out of his wrecked plane that had burrowed deep into the ground.

Two German guards with machine pistols got on board the boxcar and pulled the door closed. Without any ventilation and crowded with human bodies, the odor in the car was unbearable. It was a stinking sweat box. Everyone scrambled for a place near the door or along the sidewall of the car. Woody was not a bit bashful about making room for the four of us on the far side wall. There was not enough room for everyone to sit, so we elected to take turns.

Chapter 3

The freight train finally jerked to a start and moved slowly out of the yard. The foul dust rose from the floor in a choking mass. After several short stops the train finally got moving. An enterprising airmen started a conversation with the guards and after offering them cigarettes, one of the Germans agreed to crack open the door. This provided some relief from the stifling stench that engulfed the forty men. We had food, but there was no water. No room to lie down and no toilet facilities except for a slop bucket at each end of the car. By nightfall it became a living hell. Most of the men cursed and bitched and some were on the verge of tears. The guy that was holding up better than anyone else was Colonel McNickle who kept a constant cheerful dialogue going. He made most of the men look like a bunch of crybabies. Watching him, I felt there was little to bitch about.

It got so cold that night, we were forced to close the door and suffer with the horrible smell. We managed to get a couple hours of sleep by switching places. When morning came, the urge to urinate became unbearable. The two slop buckets were full to overflowing. Finally, a big American airman pushed the German guard aside, cracked the door, and relieved himself. The rest of us followed in military order.

The thirst for water grew with intensity when the heat of the day and the swirling dust returned. There were several among us, and that definitely included Woody, who were ready to take on the guards regardless of the risk and bail out of this hell. But we were restrained by a full colonel who realized revolt was close at hand and he made his military presence known.

Colonel Delmar Spivey was in our boxcar. He was the officer that objected to getting on the train. As far as I knew, he was the first Eighth Air Force full colonel to be taken prisoner. Shot down on the Gelsenkirchen raid, the colonel was probably in his early forties and had suffered a serious injury when the Fortress he was on crash landed. He, like McNickle, succeeded in keeping some semblance of order in the boxcar. Because of his rank and age, most of the younger men looked to him with respect and for leadership. His calm mature influence probably stopped any reckless ideas some of the men had and undoubtedly prevented a real slaughter.

In addition to the guards in the boxcars, there were others on the roofs with mounted machine guns and more German soldiers in the baggage car for additional back-up in case of an attempted escape. Had it not been for the colonel, there might have been a riot and an attempted takeover. The guards looked like they wouldn't hesitate to use their weapons.

Later that morning, the freight train pulled off on a siding, apparently to let a military or passenger train pass. Colonel Spivey got hold of the English-speaking German guard and after prolonged discussion, the Nazi major agreed to let the POWs get out of the freight cars. All of us jumped down and stood on the rough stones of the rail bed in our stocking feet, trying to work the stiffness and soreness out of our bodies. We were surround by thirty or forty guards with their machine pistols.

Large buckets of water materialized and were drained repeatedly by the thirsty men. The Germans also allowed twenty men at time to go into the pine forest to relieve themselves. Three giggling German girls watched the Americans from a short distance away, but failed to distract the Americans from nature's call.

We reluctantly boarded the boxcars after a two-hour delay of soaking up the cool, refreshing air of a beautiful day in early September 1943.

The second night passed as miserably as the first with more bitching and griping. Amazingly, Colonel McNickle still sat there without uttering one complaining word. We learned from the guards that after departing Frankfurt, the train passed through Fulda, Erfurt, and Chemnitz. From the little we could see, there was no bomb damage to the factories we passed this far inside of Germany. But it wouldn't be long before the Allied bombers would hit targets this far and even further into the German heartland.

We arrived the following day about noon at the small town of Sagan and what a relief it was to get off that filthy train. *Now if I could satisfy my thirst and bathe,* I thought, *it might not be too bad.* Water to drink and wash in. I vowed that never again would I take water for granted.

The camp was about one hundred kilometers southeast of Berlin, just south of Sagan in Silesia. It was near Poland on the river Bobr a branch of the Oder River. The area surrounding the camp was a pine forest. Each tree appeared to be planted at a precise distance apart and lined up perfectly. The area beneath the trees was completely bare with no foreign matter or trash of any kind. But the trees still looked withered and scrubby. Apparently the soil was not conducive to producing healthy trees. After reclaiming our shoes, one hundred fifty-eight prisoners (two apparently didn't make it), now known as *Kriegies* (short for *Kriegsgefangenen*), prisoners of war, marched off through the orderly pine forest to Stalag Luft III, our permanent POW camp.

We emerged from a narrow road and walked along a fence that housed a well-organized and clean military compound. For a moment, I'm sure, most of us assumed that it was our destination. But when we saw only German soldiers, we realized it was a military camp known as the *Kommandantur*. We were stopped at the entrance to the *Vorlager*, a group of several buildings outside the Allied prisoner of war camp. There the escorting guards turned over papers and the prisoners to the guards at the gate. Our new guards opened the gates and as we passed through, we were told to form in a line of fours to be counted.

After being assembled in the *Vorlager*, we were taken past some prefabricated wooden barracks to a large building. There, twenty POWs were counted and directed into the building to be processed while the others waited. When my crew and I were finally called into the building, we were searched, photographed, finger printed, and given a POW number. "*Kriegsgefangenen,* Number 2147" was my new identity on an ID card with my picture. I must admit that after two days in the boxcar I looked every bit the raunchy and sinister-looking convict my picture portrayed. Just like the Big House. I was told later that the Germans purposely took pictures of POWs after their long trips in filthy boxcars and posted them for the purpose of supporting their propaganda about American airmen that we truly were *Luft* gangsters. The German people were also told that after completing our tour of twenty-five missions of terror bombing, our government gave us a farm with a house and hundred acres of land.

We received an issue of underwear and socks from the clothing supply room, probably from the Red Cross, although, most of the clothing was British army issue. Apparently our Red Cross organization hadn't established a procedure for getting American GI clothes to us. The Germans provided a mattress cover, a coarse sheet, two blankets, a small towel, and a cooking pot and eating utensils. Then, finally, we were led into a large shower room where we gratefully shed the filth of the past forty-eight hours.

The pleasure and enjoyment of the shower, however, was ruined by the shouting of a German guard who screamed at us during the entire operation, and allowed only three minutes of warm and one minute of cold water, all done with typical German precision. We then dressed, after being deloused, in clean underclothes. It was amazing how the normal things we are accustomed to doing each day can be so much more be appreciated under such a dire situation.

It was late afternoon before we were marched to the main gate of the Center Compound, where again we were held and counted. Inside the fence I could see the prisoners gathering around the camp entrance to welcome the new arrivals. They were yelling and cheering, calling out names and shouting robust jokes. What a welcome. Even under these most dismal circumstances it was a wonderful feeling being greeted by your comrades. Misery certainly loves company. But it was heartfelt and helped to strip away some of the bitterness and despondency of the journey here.

While waiting to enter the camp, I looked at the fence surrounding the compound and it seemed even more formidable than the one at Dulag. Here again were two parallel fences, twelve feet high, separated by a maze of concertina four feet high. A very depressing and discouraging sight. My moment of exhilaration soon dissipated. *Escape!* I thought, *I've got to get out of here. Someway, somehow and quickly.*

Inside the compound we were swarmed over by the old *Kriegies*. They were dressed in all manner of clothing. The accents were from all over America and Great Britain, Australia, Canada, and many other places. I saw many former comrades from the 91st and several of my flying school classmates from other bomb groups. It was like old home week. Brown, Fountain, and others, along with their crews from the 401st, were there to greet us. I'd seen them go down and to know they were alive and okay was most gratifying. Ken Brown grabbed me, and said, "We've got room for you all in our combine in Block 51." After much backslapping and handshaking, my crew and I were led off to our assigned hut.

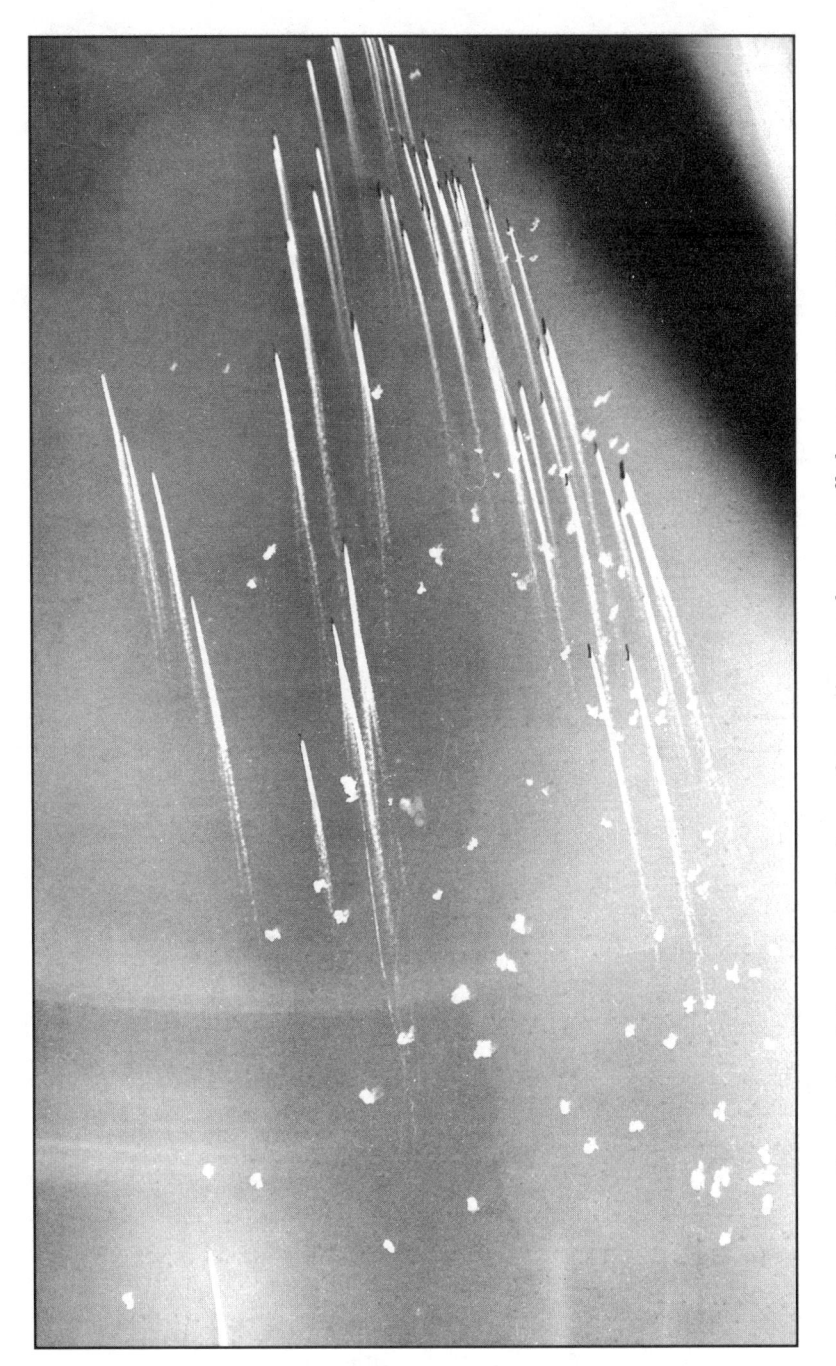

Contrails of American Fortress formation and enemy flak en route to target

Fortress hit by enemy fighters

B-17 completely blown apart by flak

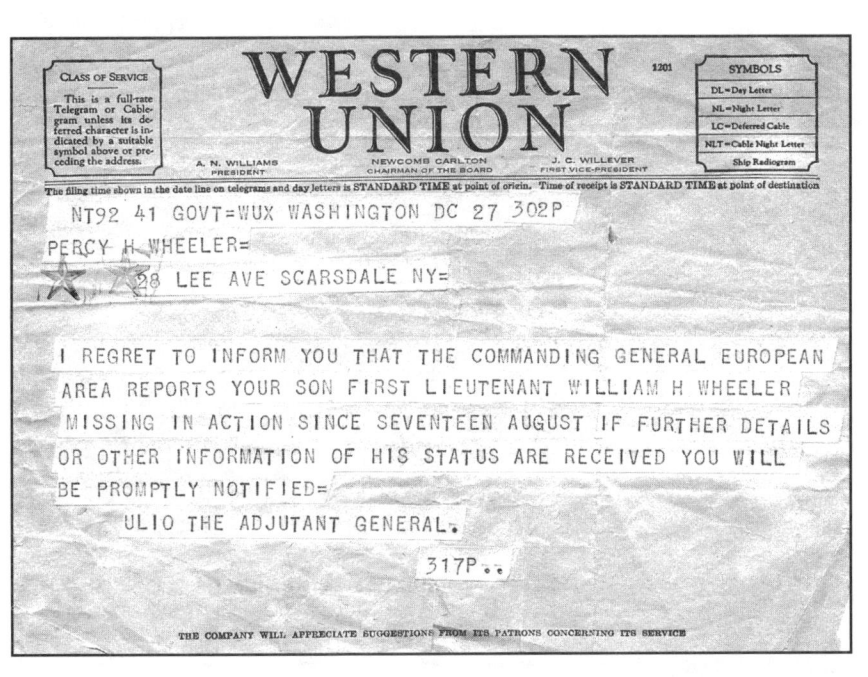

```
WESTERN UNION

NT92 41 GOVT=WUX WASHINGTON DC 27 302P
PERCY H WHEELER=
    28 LEE AVE SCARSDALE NY=

I REGRET TO INFORM YOU THAT THE COMMANDING GENERAL EUROPEAN
AREA REPORTS YOUR SON FIRST LIEUTENANT WILLIAM H WHEELER
MISSING IN ACTION SINCE SEVENTEEN AUGUST IF FURTHER DETAILS
OR OTHER INFORMATION OF HIS STATUS ARE RECEIVED YOU WILL
BE PROMPTLY NOTIFIED=
    ULIO THE ADJUTANT GENERAL.
        317P
```

Telegram notifying author's father that son is MIA

Courtesy of the Author

Captured airmen on their way to German POW camp—Dulag

POW transport—German boxcars (40 *hommes* or 8 *chevaux*)

Author's POW identification card

Courtesy of the Author

Outside looking in on Stalag III

Overview of Stalag III, *from the left*: West, North, South *(below)*, *Kommandantur*, Center and East Compounds, and the German *Vorlager (above)*

Guard tower, or Goon box

Typical *Kriegie* combine

Chapter 4
Center Compound

The Center Camp was planned to accommodate sixteen hundred prisoners and it was built as close to the minimum specifications of the Geneva Convention as any compound at Stalag Luft III. There were twelve barracks, one of which was designated as a theater or chapel, and two cookhouses. The theater had a large stage with an orchestra pit—most unusual. The huts, built far better than those in other compounds, had double walls and floors, and were one hundred twenty feet long and thirty feet wide. Each hut was divided into two large rooms sufficient to accommodate seventy men, and two small rooms at each end of the building. One contained a small kitchen with a small cookstove, the other was used as a night latrine. The block commander occupied the small rooms on the other end of the barracks. Each of the large rooms had a coal-burning stove or Nuremberg heater, but there was seldom sufficient coal to keep it fired. There were also four pit-latrines, twenty seaters, for use during the day. The camp had been occupied by NCOs until June 1943 when all but fifty enlisted men were moved out of the Center Camp to Stalag Luft VI.

At the time of our arrival there were three compounds at Stalag Luft III—the Center, East, and North—and the Germans had planned to use the POW camp for Allied air force officers only.

My first impression of the camp was very disappointing. It looked so dilapidated and disorderly, so different from the German *Kommandantur*. Windows were broken and doors hung on one hinge. This was certainly not what we had expected. We'd been told that because we were air force officers, Marshall Hermann Göring would provide us with special accommodations far better than those for other captive servicemen. If this was the best, one could only imagine what the other camps must be like. A country club it was not, far from it. The swimming pool turned out to be a muddy pool in the center of the compound, used for fighting fires. The huts were dirty, some of the electrical wiring was torn out, wood framing was taken from the latrine and barracks, and some of the bunks had few or no slats to hold the mattresses. Most of the prisoners wore beards, the clothes they wore were a mixture of uniforms of several nationalities, and some of the men looked like they hadn't bathed in weeks.

Apparently the NCOs had caused considerable damage to the camp in the short time they occupied it. The wood siding stripped from the buildings was used for firewood and the barracks were left in a ravaged condition. The Germans wouldn't make repairs and the enlisted men refused to work.

The huts were much like those in the Dulag Luft. To afford some form of separation in the two large rooms, each combine was walled off with six double-decker bunks and wooden wall lockers, which gave them some privacy. The prisoners were given their own rations and could prepare their food individually. Generally the meals were prepared for ten or twelve men in the combine. They shared their Red Cross food and the German rations. Each *Kriegie* took turns cooking, unless one was so bad that the others would not eat the food he prepared. The camp appeared disorganized, dilapidated, and dirty. It was a grave disappointment knowing that we'd be confined in such a place for an indefinite period of time. But it did strengthen my determination to escape.

At the time, a Major McMillian was the senior American in the camp. The majority of the flying officers were British, Canadians, and Australians. Squadron Leader Pritcher, a POW for two and a half years, was the senior officer in the camp.

I was told that Lieutenant Brunn was the American contact on the X Committee, which was organized and operated by the British. I contacted him and was told to wait until they organized the next project and I would be assigned to it, but for the present there was nothing planned. It was a real letdown for me, hoping to get in on some escape plan immediately and get back to England. Some of the RAF men had been in the camp since November of 1939 and no one had successfully escaped from Stalag Luft III and got back to England. Difficult as it seemed, I was determined to try, and believed that it was possible. I just had to believe it could be done. In the meantime, I'd find out as much as possible about escaping, and plan my effort in that direction The initial pleasure and enthusiasm of meeting some of my comrades soon faded.

Four weeks passed with no word from Mary or home, and as yet no entry into the X organization. I became very disheartened and the bleak outlook of spending months behind barbed wire became obsessively dismal. The lack of organization and purpose in the camp did little to improve my disposition. The greatest effort and activity of the POWs seemed to be doing anything they could think of that would frustrate and annoy the Germans.

There were two formations or as the Germans called it, *Appell*, a day. Its primary purpose was to count the prisoners. To the German High Command, *Appell* was the most important function of the camp supervisors. The exact numbers had to be tallied twice a day of all the thousands of prisoners held in Germany. One missing prisoner would cause grave concern throughout the camps, and a recount and search would continue until the numbers were reconciled. The *Kriegies* would form up by huts or blocks in the large open area in the middle of the compound. We would stand five deep while the German sergeant walked in front of the men and counted us. Frequently some POW would hide for the hell of it and not appear for *Appell*. That caused the other prisoners more discomfort than the Germans, since they would stay outside in formation until the absent prisoner was found.

The Canadians and the Australians were the worst. Any aggravation, regardless how large or small it was, if it annoyed the Germans, it was a victory to them. Several of them appeared for *Appell* one morning without pants or undershorts. Each time the German sergeant counting the prisoners came to one of the exposed *Kriegies*, he would lose his concentration and have to start the count all over. Most *Kriegies* enjoyed the show of defiance. But aside from a good laugh, little was accomplished.

The camp *Kommandant Oberst* (Colonel) Friedrich von Lindeiner-Wildau was a perfect example of a Prussian officer. A man in his early sixties, he had served in World War I, and apparently served with honor as indicated by his decorations. It was rumored that he disliked the Nazi regime and despised Hitler and shortly after they came to power he left Germany. However, in 1937, he was called back for duty and like most good Germans returned to serve his country at the prospect of the coming war. The heavy burden of his duties for more than four years had seriously affected his health. He also became disenchanted over the atrocities the Germans were inflicting on Europe and requested retirement for medical reasons. He was refused and reassigned as commandant of Stalag Luft. in the spring of 1942. Von Lindeiner-Wildau was quite tall and stood very erect and looked every inch the typical German officer of the old school as he walked to the center of the parade ground. He would appear alternately at *Appell* in each compound, usually with two brown dachshunds running and yelping alongside him.

One morning the Canadians in the hut next to ours started to whistle the tune of "the worms crawl in, the worms crawl out" in step with the *Kommandant* as he walked to the center of the compound. The German officer stopped, turned sharply, and walked across the compound directly to the group of hecklers. He stopped six feet in front of the Canadians and silently stared at them. The whistling gradually diminished in volume and within a matter of seconds ended abruptly. Satisfied that he had made his point, he turned around smartly and walked briskly to the center of the compound. The little scene was most impressive, and I had to admire the German for the way he handled the situation.

Many of the American POWs appeared to literally accept the German adage "for you the war is over," and sacked out on their bunks and did nothing. They seemed to have no interest in doing anything. Just lie back and wait for war's end. By the end of September 1943, most POWs were convinced that the war would be over by the coming Christmas.

The Center Compound had a chapel, and a chaplain was available to conduct religious services. The attendance was quite small, not only because of the lack of seating but of interest. This changed dramatically on the arrival of Padre Murdo Ewen MacDonald, a minister of the Church of England who served the British camps and volunteered to visit the American compounds. He spoke with a rich and strong Scottish accent. When it was known that he was giving a sermon in our camp, there was always a mad rush after *Appell* to get a seat in the chapel. Padre McDonald could really get a wonderful grip on you to where you would completely forget about your depressing and dismal surroundings and precarious predicament. He was a truly magnificent preacher.

There was also a library and several educational classes were in progress. The YMCA provided musical instruments and all sorts of athletic equipment. The British played football and rugby almost daily with great enthusiasm and vigor. But it seemed that only a small percentage of the Americans took advantage of these activities. I counted myself among the majority, because all I could think about was escaping. I spent endless hours walking the inside perimeter like a caged animal. I did, however, enroll in a German language course, thinking it would help me if I got away.

At the time, the British were running the show, but like everything else in the camp there appeared to be a lack of organization. Anytime the Americans got involved in an escape project, it was done in such great haste and without proper planning that it was inevitably unsuccessful. Life in the Center Camp was just plain miserable.

That all changed, however, about four weeks after my arrival at Stalag Luft III. We were told that the Americans would occupy and control the Center Compound and Colonel Spivey would become our new senior officer. He and three other colonels—Kennedy, Jenkins and Stillman—were sent from the North Camp to organize our compound. The rapid expansion of the American Air Forces combat groups in England and their increased bombing activity resulted in a great influx of American POWs. More space was needed and the Germans wanted to separate the Americans from the other Allied POWs. It was to their advantage because they believed the older English prisoners were influencing the newcomers and it was causing them more problems. True, the Americans learned a lot from the British, not only about escape activity and smuggling, but more importantly, survival. However, some of the Americans had been interned for a year or more. Most of the longtimers had been shot down in North Africa, some as early as the summer of 1942. The older American

Kriegies had acquired a significant amount of knowledge from the British and believed they were capable of taking care of themselves. The Geneva Convention also required that POWs be segregated by nationality.

The oldest American prisoner in our camp was a naval flyer, Lieutenant James Dunne, captured in March 1942. He was flying off a carrier in the North Sea and got lost. The Germans located him, gave him a bearing to Holland, and then shot him down. Jimmy had his own agenda and did not participate to any great degree in camp activity. We all envied Dunne because he had a complete dress uniform and would generally stand *Appell* in his dress blues, gold braid and garrison hat.

Colonel Delmar Spivey had arrived with us from Dulag Luft but was sent to the North Compound, which at that time was occupied by Americans and other Allied prisoners, but mainly British officers. Spivey, a tall, slender, balding man, and a West Pointer, was the man who had somehow controlled our anger throughout the horrible ride in the boxcar.

It was not understood why the Germans had sent him to the North Compound initially with other ranking officers that came with us in the boxcars. Fortunately for us, they did and Spivey made exceptional good use of the few weeks he spent in the North Compound, where he met a West Point classmate of his, Colonel Charles Goodrich.

Goodrich had arrived in Stalag Luft III in March 1943 and was the senior American officer (SAO) in the North Compound. Although he outranked Wing Commander Day, the senior British officer, he was content to serve under him and learn everything possible about life in a prison camp from Day, the most experienced senior POW in Stalag Luft III. The two men became good friends and soon Goodrich was given carte blanche to all the knowledge, secret information, and experience the British had acquired in the organization and operation of the prison camp. Colonel Goodrich would soon be designated the SAO of the newly built South Compound, scheduled to open in late September 1943 for American officers only. But before Goodrich left, he passed on to Colonel Spivey all the information he acquired from the RAF on camp administration, operations, and clandestine activities.

The separation of the Allied and American airmen was acceptable to both the Germans and the Americans. Although the senior American officers understood that it was against US doctrine to cooperate with the Germans, they agreed to go along with the plan, mainly because they could exercise better control and supervision over the Americans. And further, to establish a level of military discipline that they considered necessary to meet reasonable standards and conduct befitting American officers.

Accordingly, the British and other RAF types were moved out of the Center to the North and East Camps, leaving the Center and the South exclusively to the Americans. The change in the operation of the camp was felt almost immediately, and the attitude of the American POWs improved noticeably. The men were told to clean themselves, encouraged to shave off beards, cut their hair, and participate in the new shower program, a concession that Colonel Spivey had won from the *Kommandant*. Saturday morning inspections of all personnel and their living quarters were scheduled and conducted much to the dismay of many *Kriegies*. Education classes and craft courses, those permitted by the Germans, were started and attendance was encouraged. Athletic competition between blocks (huts) was organized and physical exercise sessions were made mandatory. An orchestra and a drama club were formed under an Entertainment Committee. An interviewing group found a wide range of professionals among the POWs and the greatest cross section of talent imaginable. Teachers, big band musicians, actors, writers, professional athletes, engravers, even an admitted forger who was very helpful in producing German travel permits and documents. The initial interviewing of all new prisoners also accomplished a most essential function. The Germans were known to insert stooges into the camp. They were highly trained men, spoke perfect English, and knew all the familiar American characteristics, habits, and background information of the person they were impersonating. A new prisoner had to be cleared by an Intelligence Committee before he could take part in camp activities. Usually it was a matter of being identified by a friend or member of his combat organization.

The camp was organized along military lines. Colonel Spivey had an adjutant and a staff, each hut had a block commander and each combine had a leader. *Appell* were held as military formations with formal reporting and issuing of orders. Some of the older prisoners objected to the new procedures, saying it only helped the Germans by making their job easier. These individuals maintained that it was the prisoners' duty to do everything they could to disrupt the enemy. However, Colonel Spivey and the senior officers believed that their responsibility was to maintain the highest possible level of morale among the POWs, keeping them mentally and physically intact until they were returned to US military control. The colonel said that if in any way his actions were counter to accepted military behavior, he would take full responsibility and suffer the consequences after the war.

Most agreed and supported the new regime and considered it a great improvement over the former method. Our combine in Hut 51 consisted of my crew and Brown's and Wilson's crews and I was duly elected the combine leader. I immediately set up a duty roster and encouraged our roommates to participate in the numerous programs that had been started.

Our block commander was Captain Sam Magee whose story was rather unique and repressively sad. He was a B-25 navigator on the Dolittle raid on Tokyo in April 1942 and was one of the lucky ones who made it back. He bailed out over China, was picked up by friendly farmers, and returned to US military control. The air force felt that he had done his part and assigned him to safe duty in the Training Command to teach gunnery. However, it happened to be the same organization that Colonel Spivey commanded. The colonel knew that if they were going to teach young recruits how to shoot, the instructors should have some actual combat experience. So he, Colonels Kennedy and Jenkins along with Captain Magee traveled to England and volunteered to fly a combat mission as observers with the Eighth Air Force. Ironically, they chose the Gelsenkirchen raid on 12 August, a very hazardous raid into the Ruhr Valley. The raid was a complete disaster and an absolute snafu. I flew the mission and was damn lucky to get back. Not so for the two Fortresses with the high-ranking observers aboard. Ominously both aircraft were shot down and once again Sam Magee took to his parachute, bailed out and was captured immediately. Sam was not a very happy warrior.

The "X" organization was disbanded which upset me. But I was told that it was being reorganized under a new American team and I would be a part of the group. In the meantime, the training I had received while at Bovington during my two weeks at the Combat Crew Replacement Center was put to use. I had been taught to send coded messages back in my personal letters. This gave me a certain amount of satisfaction, but my heart was still set on escaping.

Each prisoner was allowed to send two letters and four post cards a month. The letter forms were white-lined paper approximately six inches wide and twelve inches long, folded in three equal parts to form an envelope. My first letters were to Mary and my mother. Most letters I sent home or to Mary had coded information in them that was passed to me by the Intelligence Committee.

Chapter 5
Escape Attempt

In October, the first serious American escape plan was organized and implemented. It was to be a tunnel two hundred eighty-seven feet long, starting from a half-empty block closest to the southern fence. The location of the Center Compound made tunneling difficult as it was surrounded on all three sides by the East Camp, the *Vorlager* and the *Kommandantur*. The southside of the compound was bordered by the pine forest. The area immediately beyond the fence was cleared of trees for at least fifty feet. But the dense pine forest beyond the cleared area provided the best cover for an escape. However, the closest hut to the fence was over two hundred feet away from it. It would be a long dig, but the Americans were very optimistic. They decided on a blitz operation with the accent placed on speed rather than a well-planned and properly constructed tunnel. The Americans reasoned that if it was to be successful, they had to get out before the cold weather to give the escapees a better chance of survival.

My first assignment in the escape effort was with the security group, an elaborate organization that covered the entire camp. Its purpose was to know exactly where every German guard was every minute of the day. A number of creative signals was put in place to warn of the approach of guards and in particular the ones called ferrets. These German guards, members of the *Abwehr*, were highly trained individuals who roamed the compound. They would walk outside the huts and stop by open windows or hide in the buildings to listen. The ferrets would squirm under the huts or up between the ceiling and the roof to spy. They professed not to understand or speak English, but they hid in every conceivable place in an effort to overhear any talk of escape activity. Frequently, the guards would arrive at first light and roust everyone out of a suspected hut, before the *Kriegies* had a chance to have their morning coffee and toast, to search the building. The POWs would be kept outside while the ferrets searched through their food, clothing, and personal belongings, literally tearing bunks apart, removing boards and leaving everything spread about. They were by far the most hated of the Germans guards.

On any tunnel project, dispersal of the sand was the major problem. An elaborate plan was devised to dig garbage pits and prepare the soil for a vegetable garden in the spring. The plan was presented to the German *Kommandant*, who approved it and authorized the use of shovels. However, the tools were carefully counted and returned at day's end. The moist sand removed from the tunnel was much darker than the sandy soil on the surface of the ground, so to conceal the sand removed from the tunnel, it had to be buried in pits and covered with surface sand. As the elevation of the ground under the gardens rose noticeably and concealment became obvious, other means of disposal became necessary. Several methods were used, spreading the sand on top of the ceiling boards in the huts and dispersing it in small quantities around the camp. This was accomplished by scattering the sand in the court while a volleyball game was in progress or letting it pour down one's leg while walking the perimeter. A sausage-like sack or stocking with a hole at the bottom was hung from the *Kriegie*'s waist and down the inside of his pants leg. The sand would slowly pour down his leg, like grains of sand in an hourglass, as he walked and it become mixed with the surface soil. One great asset was the available manpower. Regardless of how primitive or menial the tasks, we had the men to do it.

Two weeks into the operation, I was offered the opportunity to join the men digging the tunnel. Once a *Kriegie* was assigned to the digging team, his chances of being selected in the first group to escape if the tunnel was successful improved considerably. To succeed in getting at least a few men back safely to England, it was necessary to limit the number that could leave when the tunnel was completed. The selection process was strictly controlled by the X Committee. First priority went to those that were most capable of getting back. These select men had to be in good physical and mental condition and preferably speak the German language. Next were the longtimers and those that contributed most to the escape activity. The last group, which I would be in, was selected by drawing straws. The number of first-night escapees was limited to the number of available forged German papers and sets of civilian clothing. If the selected groups got away clean, then it would be open to anyone who wanted to go it alone, regardless of how well prepared he was. I would be among the latter group. However, once the prisoners got away and were missing at the next *Appell*, the Germans would literally tear the camp apart until they found the tunnel, regardless of how long it would take.

The work on the tunnel was done mainly at night so the POWs on the digging team would move into the hut where the tunnel originated each evening before lockup. The following morning the diggers would return and assemble with their own blocks for the count at *Appell*. The entrance to the tunnel was well concealed beneath the hut's heavy Nuremberg cooking stove. The stove was removed from the brick base it rested on and the base was hollowed out. The huts were set off the ground by two-foot pillars, which made it easy for the German ferrets to crawl under them. However, the weight of the stoves required a brick-and-mortar foundation set in the ground that provided an excellent entry for a tunnel. The stove could be replaced quickly by two men with two sturdy poles placed around the stove's waist, whether it was in use or not. During an alert, the stove and bricks could be replaced in a matter of minutes. The entrance to the tunnel was so well disguised that it would take someone with a magnifying glass to detect its location.

The vertical shaft leading down to the tunnel was about four feet square and fifteen feet deep. At the bottom of the shaft was a shored-up room about eight feet square, high enough for a man to sit upright. This area was used to store sand temporarily, accommodate two men working the bellows and as a rest area. The lateral tunnel began from this room. My first night in the tunnel was kind of scary and I had second thoughts about continuing that form of work. The tunnel was no more than three feet in diameter, just enough room to crawl through on your elbows and knees. The digger with a crude shovel, more like a scoop made of tin cans, would crawl in first and cut away at the moist sand ahead of him. He would then push the sand back along the sides of his body to the fellow behind him, who was facing the opposite direction. He would pull the dirt to his front and load it on a crude sled. The sled would then be pulled back to the base of the tunnel and the sand loaded into sacks and hauled up to the floor of the hut. The tunnel was about thirty feet long when I first entered it.

After my briefing, I was handed the scoop and told to start digging. I remembered digging tunnels as a kid so it didn't seem to be a problem. The only light came from a piece of cloth floating like a wick in melted German margarine set in a shallow sardine tin. I pushed my meager torch ahead as I squirmed the first ten feet or so into the tunnel. *Not too bad*, I thought.

But as I crawled down the passageway, my mind began to work against my brave intentions. My greatest fear was of a cave-in and being smothered. There was no shoring in the tunnel, just moist, sandy walls. The rescue drill in case of a cave-in was rather optimistic. "Be calm, don't panic and we'll dig you out." As I crawled further into the tunnel, a severe case of claustrophobia seized me. I started to sweat, my mouth became dry, and I had a hard time breathing. I stopped and felt the guy's foot behind me. On the verge of panic I wanted to back out. I felt as though my lungs were collapsing for lack of air.

The guy behind me called, "What's the matter, Wheeler?"

I sucked in some air and replied, "Nothing. Just that it's pretty hard to breathe down here."

My digging partner replied, "Yeah, there's not much air, but you'll get used to it. Just take it easy."

I forcefully and grudgingly shoved my fear aside and crawled on. The further into the tunnel I crawled, the more closed in and frightening it became. Pushing onward, I reached the end. There, I settled myself down, trying to breathe slower, and started to dig. Our two-man team was required to cut through the earth to increase the tunnel by at least four feet. The fear finally left me and I went to work in earnest.

After each designated section of the tunnel to be dug was completed, the diggers would crawl out to rest and the tunnel expert would sight the tunnel to be sure it was true and straight. The digger and loader would then change places and that would constitute a shift. I worked on the tunnel for six straight nights and was then given two days off. The fear lessened but not completely. The feeling of suffocation was hard to ignore.

Air was pumped down a pipe from the bellows in the base room. The pipe was made of tin cans, about two inches in diameter. The lips of the cans were bent back and then joined together to form a long tube. The tube was then wrapped in newspaper and buried in the sand along the bottom of the tunnel. It was quite an ingenious rig and it helped, but not much. It required two well-conditioned *Kriegies* to keep the air flowing by manually pumping the bellows.

The tunnel was going exceptionally well and everyone on the project was exceedingly optimistic about it. There were a couple of minor cave-ins, but no one was hurt and the questionable areas were shored up. The tunnel was about one hundred fifty feet long, estimated to be better than halfway to the exit. The dispersal of sand was becoming more difficult and some of the spreaders were getting careless by dumping the dark-colored sand in conspicuous places. Several tons of sand were spread over the ceiling boards and other huts were being used as well.

Another major problem of tunneling was getting wood for shoring. Each POW was allowed eight bed slats to hold his mattress and there were no replacements. The Germans knew what they were used for, and they were carefully controlled. The boards, made of hardwood and just the right length, were ideal for shoring. Most prisoners working on escape projects slept on as few as four or five slats. When shoring was needed, a call went out for donations and usually they got what was needed. Uncooperative *Kriegies* would usually end up with less than four slats. Some were extracted even as the unobliging prisoners slept.

Digging of the tunnel came to a sudden and devastating end when a massive amount of sand came cascading down onto an inquisitive ferret. The German, walking through the hut, noticed a few grains of sand on the floor. He stopped, looked up, and must have seen the source. Standing on a bench, he poked his metal rod through a crack between the ceiling boards. At that moment the ceiling boards gave way and several hundred pounds of sand poured down on the ferret knocking him off the bench and onto the floor. He was unhurt but very mad.

Once the Germans suspected a tunnel, the Goon Squads were brought in, usually about twenty or thirty soldiers with machine pistols, and all the POWs were ordered out of their huts, to form up and be counted. Then the German escape experts marched in and would go through every inch of the camp. The *Kriegies* were kept outside in formation, regardless of the weather, until the tunnel was found. When it was located, they would bring in the fire truck and flood the tunnel with water. All the ingenious paraphernalia devised by the POWs was collected, documented, and then displayed by the Germans in their museum in the *Vorlager*. The Germans were very proud of this display and of their record of foiling countless escape attempts. The museum was the first stop for any visiting dignitary.

Our tunnel was a bust, but I had made my first effort and even though it failed, I felt good. Having overcome my fear of working underground, I was ready to do it again. I had made my contribution and was now completely accepted into the X organization. There would be more attempts.

Chapter 6
First Letters

My first letter arrived about ten weeks after I was shot down and it was from Mary. She told me she called Clyde Gillespie, my squadron commander, that awful night when I hadn't arrived in London, and he told her that Buster Peek's crew reported seeing several chutes open as my plane was going down. She also said that she sent a telegram the day after I was shot down to my mother assuring her that she truly believed that I was alive and was being held as a prisoner of war. Much later she heard through the Red Cross, confirming her optimism, that I had been captured. She also told me that my promotion to captain came through a few days after I was shot down. She reaffirmed her love for me and said she would wait, no matter how long.

The letter from Mary seemed to bring us together again. Up until that time, I felt alone and that somehow our affair seemed unreal, a fantasy like a wonderful dream that ended when I hit the ground in Germany and was taken prisoner. But it had been real and now I was more determined than ever to get out and back to England.

* * * *

I did not call Mary the following weekend as I'd promised. Instead I went to London with Norman. There I met an attractive, blonde Greek woman named Sylvia at the Astor. She was married, but her husband was still in Greece while she lived in a luxurious flat in Bayswater. She was a very accommodating young woman who thought all Americans were marvelous.

That Sunday night on the train returning to my base at Bovington, I realized my weekend was nothing compared to the one I'd spent with Mary. I missed her and regretted not seeing her. I also reproached myself for not being honest and telling her about my commitment to another woman in America. The following weekend, however, I decided to call Mary and tell her about Clare. Mary agreed to meet me at her flat Saturday afternoon at one o'clock. I arrived late and half bombed, two character flaws that Mary considered unforgivable. When my friends and I arrived in London we had opened the bar at the Regency Place Hotel and stayed until closing. After a lengthy apology and a gift of a very large bunch of heather for being more than an hour late, Mary finally forgave me, well—almost.

We spent afternoon feeding ducks in St. James Park and sight-seeing. Mary had been quite subdued, certainly nothing like the vivacious and exuberant girl I remembered from our previous time together. I wasn't sure whether it was because of my late arrival or drinking. But something was bothering her and it continued through dinner that evening. After dinner at Hackett's, I insisted that we go to the Astor thinking it might improve her disposition. It didn't. I was certain that she wasn't at all happy being with me and was surprised when I dropped her off at her flat and she invited me in.

She made coffee and we sat together on her sofa drinking it. After a prolonged silence, I asked her why she had been so quiet and pensive. She told me that she had visited her mother that morning, whom she hadn't seen in several months, and it was not a very pleasant encounter. She declined to elaborate and I didn't press her for details. Our conversation continued in a rather trivial and awkward vein but not for long. Before I realized what had happened, she was in my arms in a heated embrace reminiscent of our first night together. But as my desire and passion grew, I was struck with the realization that I could not make love to her. Although I sensed her willingness, I found myself incapable of physical love. It was not only because of my promise to Clare, but I just couldn't in good conscience take advantage of this lovely girl. I tried but failed to tell her why. She withdrew when she sensed my reluctance and moved away from me.

When I started to leave she surprised me by saying, "You've missed the last train to Watford. Stay the night if you like."

For some time we lay silently side by side, both fully clothed. Finally she started talking so quietly that I could hardly hear her. "When I was six years old, my mother entered me in a film contest that was being sponsored by Pontings, a West End department store. Out of twenty-five or thirty children that participated, I won and was awarded a film contract. My mother was thrilled and from that point on she pushed me relentlessly and selfishly. She was determined to make me an outstanding actress. I did quite well and made several movies with famous film stars. But when I reached adolescence and outgrew children's parts, my mother was told that I had potential, but to wait until I outgrew the awkward stage. My mother wasn't at all pleased but she did enroll me in the Royal Academy of Dramatic Arts. She missed the glamour and celebrity status of the film set and became very difficult. My mother was an alcoholic and when under the influence she became sadistic. I was constantly abused as a child and more so when my film career ended, she became excessively brutal. I had a horrible and terrifying experience when I was fourteen and I ran away. When my mother found me she sent me to a convent in Brussels." Mary stopped talking and I remained silent, thinking she would continue.

Finally she did. "I was at the convent for nearly two years, two very lonely and unhappy years. However, the discipline and treatment by the nuns helped to strengthen my character and when I returned home, I was determined to resist my mother's abusive and domineering ways. I told her I wanted to find a job and be independent. She protested and threatened me, but I was determined and got a job in a London night club. I had to lie about my age because I was only sixteen."

Mary went on to tell me about her experiences working in The Cabaret and how wonderful it was to be free of her mother's influence. While working there she met and became close friends with a beautiful showgirl named Muriel. When her mother moved back to Hempstead, she and Muriel rented a magnificent flat in Maida Vale. England was at war with Germany and the owner wanted to move to the country, so he let the two young women have his flat for only four pounds a month, just to occupy and care for it.

Mary continued, "I really enjoyed working at The Cabaret and my friendship with Muriel. My mother had discouraged any relationships, so Muriel was my first real friend. We had great times together, even during the terrible bombing, but it all came to an end when Muriel met and fell in love with a German. Their love affair came to a tragic end when he disappeared shortly after the blitz began. It was possible that he was a spy and the authorities arrested him. Muriel started drinking excessively and we finally separated. It broke my heart, but I wasn't going to live with another alcoholic like my mother."

She talked for several more minutes cradled in my arms and finally fell asleep with her head on my shoulder. I found myself completely intrigued and fascinated with this remarkable girl. I lay there, hopelessly trying to resolve my predicament between wanting her desperately and my promise to marry Clare. By morning I'd found no solution to my dilemma. I left her without telling her why I wouldn't see her again but I promised to call.

Forming up for *Appell*

Preparing dinner on Nuremberg stove

Contents of American Red Cross parcel

Colonel Delmar T. Spivey

Courtesy U.S. Air Force
Academy Library

**Colonel Friedrich-Wilhelm
von Lindeiner**

Courtesy U.S. Air Force
Academy Library

Lieutenant Colonel
Melvin McNickle

Left to right: Lieutenant Colonel Alpert P. "Bud" Clarke,
Wing Commander Kimbal, Colonel Charles Goodrich,
and Lieutenant Colonel Dick Klocke

POW postcard containing form letter

Courtesy of the Author

August 5, 1944

Dear Mrs Wheeler, In beginning, I'm proud to say I have known your son for some time as well as served under his command for a similar period. Please convey my sincerest respects to him and certainly best wishes for his health and well being – along that all the boys and myself are coming along fine. Floyd Thompson received letters yesterday from his father telling of having heard from my mother (Mrs Lee), yourself and the other boys families. I don't remember missing a single line or incident. All of us greatly enjoyed them. I would like very much to write Bill but the present situation deems it not too plausable. Many times I wondered how he, and the others, were making out. As much as he is loved and respected by us all, I know you must be very proud of him. I need not mention his courage or gallantry in action – his record speaks for itself. His personal invitation to a re-union on returning I shall assuridly fulfill. The pleasure of meeting Bill's Mother I look to with much gladness. Sincerely – Sgt. Scurlock

**POW form letter
(to my mother from author's flight engineer)**

Courtesy of the Author

Mary's picture received while in Center Compound

Courtesy of the Author

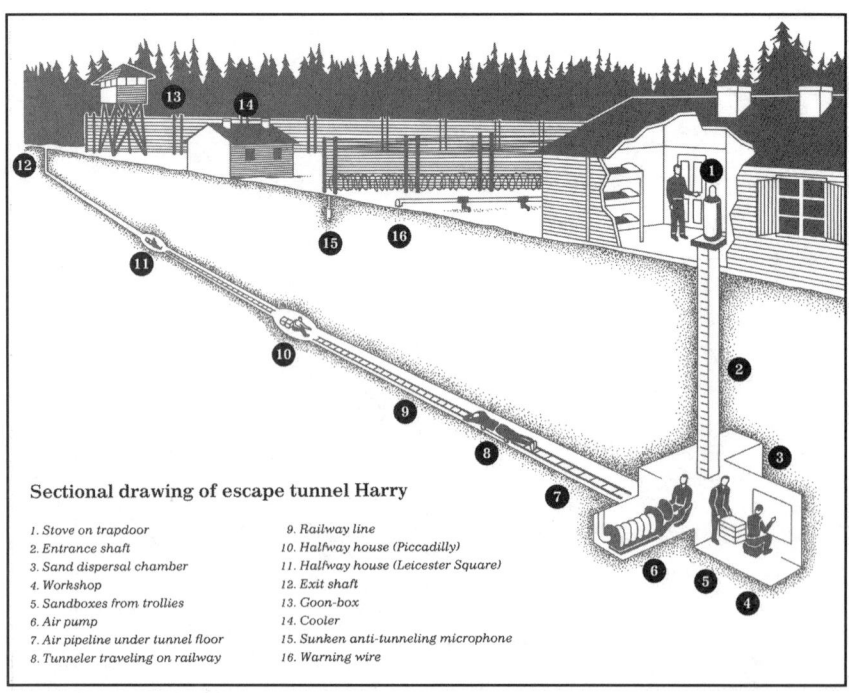

Sectional drawing of escape tunnel Harry

1. Stove on trapdoor
2. Entrance shaft
3. Sand dispersal chamber
4. Workshop
5. Sandboxes from trollies
6. Air pump
7. Air pipeline under tunnel floor
8. Tunneler traveling on railway
9. Railway line
10. Halfway house (Piccadilly)
11. Halfway house (Leicester Square)
12. Exit shaft
13. Goon-box
14. Cooler
15. Sunken anti-tunneling microphone
16. Warning wire

Sketch of the British tunnel (Harry)—North Compound

Burial of the 50 RAF airmen killed by Nazis—
captured after The Great Escape

Walking the perimeter—endless circuits

Evacuation from Stalag III, January 1945

Starting the long march

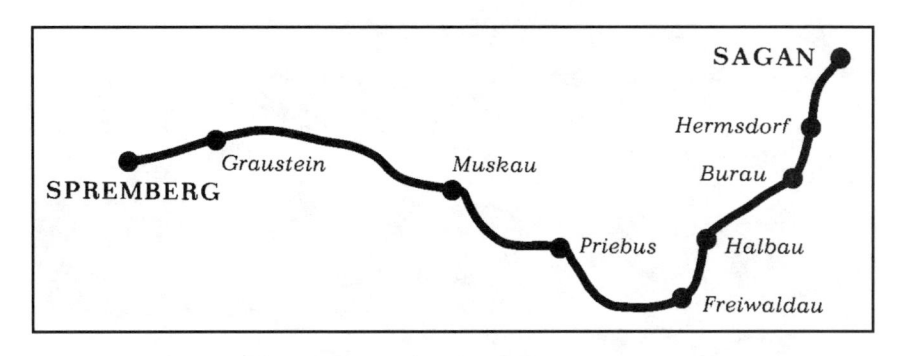

Sketches of the long march route

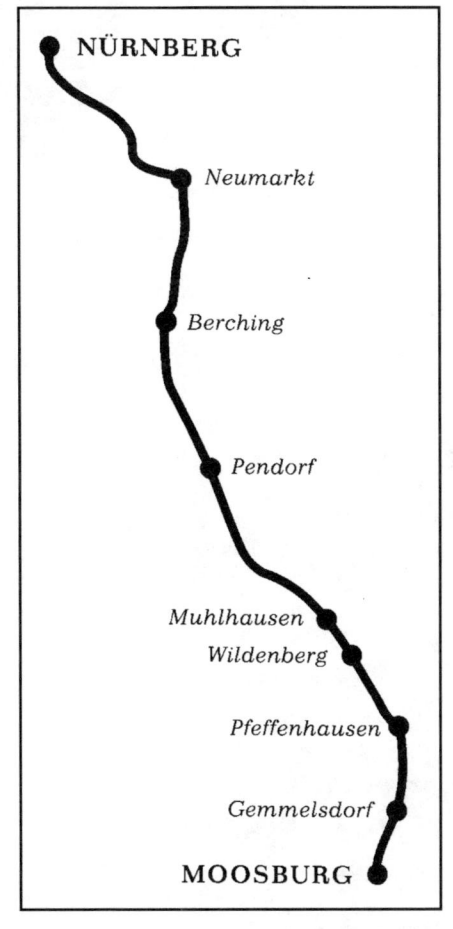

Fifteen-minute break

The author—Nuremberg,
February 1945

Courtesy of the Author

Bill Munger, to my *left*; Larry Phelan, *far left*; and fellow POWs

Courtesy of the Author

Aubrey Stanhope, *far left*, and friends

Courtesy of the Author

Stalag XIIID, Nuremberg

Chapter 7

First Christmas

Norman Retchin, a classmate and friend, was shot down in June, and he and his crew were in the South Camp. Norman sent me a note saying he had just spent two weeks in the cooler for attempted escape. He was also charged with destroying German property and for that they threatened to shoot him, which was the penalty for such a crime. And the fact that he was Jewish made the threat all the more serious. He had stripped some wood from his hut and made a ladder. His plan was to use the ladder after lockup to span the two twelve-foot fences and crawl across the area between the fences. He managed to get to the top of the first fence and halfway across the span when the ladder broke. He fell into the coils of barbed wire and had to be extracted by German guards who heard the crash and Norm's cry.

I thought about the night Norm and I drove a one-horse carriage through Marrakech, completely bombed, doing a Crosby-Hope road show, singing "On the Road to Morocco." We gave the Arab driver a big cigar and a half bottle of rum and convinced him to ride in the passenger's seat while we took over the driver's seat.

On our arrival in Marrakech we were cleared to open our secret orders that confirmed our final destination — the United Kingdom. Not North Africa or the Far East but merry old England and we were celebrating. Our festive evening was dampened somewhat by the absence of our good friend Alden "Dopey" Mann, a pilot and classmate. He had made an emergency landing in Portuguese Guinea on the African coast, a neutral country where he and his crew could have been interned for the duration. Fortunately, Colonel Harris, our CO, was onboard his aircraft and with the help of General Hap Arnold he got the crew out. However, sadly and most unfortunately, Dopey was killed last May on a mission to Kiel, Germany. His wife, Judy, was expecting their first child in June.

Thanksgiving came and as promised, I served our combine a turkey. A couple of weeks prior to the holiday, I stashed away several cans of Spam, crackers, dried milk, and eggs. That morning I secretly mixed the ingredients together and molded it in the form a large fowl and baked it. It was a work of art, but it still tasted like Spam.

The first snowfall of the winter, about six inches, came in early December and that night two fellow POWs and I attempted an escape through the fence. The Escape Committee provided us with a crude wire cutter which they believed would cut through the fence. After lockup, we left our blackout huts covered by white mattress covers and crawled through the snow toward the fence. All went well as we made our way cautiously across the open area to the southern fence. About halfway there, I heard footsteps crunching in the snow. We froze, praying that we were invisible under the camouflage covers. The German *Hundsfuehrer* stopped as his guard dog, a huge Doberman, sniffed at the guy crawling behind me. Surprisingly, the dog did not attack or even growl. The guard reached down, pulled back the cover from the *Kriegie*, and said, "*Was ist los!*" He then ordered us at gunpoint to get up and marched us straight to the gate where we were taken to the cooler. Two weeks of solitary confinement convinced me that the Germans had no sense of humor.

The days dragged by, but there was still great optimism among most prisoners. As each milestone came and went, we pushed our predictions and dreams of liberation ahead a couple more months. As Christmas came and went, we advanced our hopes to the spring, when the invasion of Europe was sure to happen. It was still a very miserable holiday, and the uncertainty and loneliness became almost unbearable. New Year's Eve, I, like many of my fellow *Kriegies*, got half-drunk on raisin-and-barley brew and for a short time the misery and depression we felt was forgotten.

At the risk of being shot, British and American prisoners climbed the fence that separated the East and Center Camps to visit each other. Fortunately the German sentries looked the other way in the spirit of the holidays and took no drastic measures. But after the drunken high vanished, most of us got sick and became more remorseful and depressed than ever.

The most disconcerting news was hearing that several Russian prisoners who had worked in the *Vorlager* had been shot. They had found the *Kommandant's* dachshunds wandering around the compound, cornered and caught the dogs, then cooked and ate them. The *Kommandant* was so outraged at the Russians, he had them shot.

The Russian prisoners were treated worse than animals. I saw one stick his finger in the hub of a horse-drawn wagon wheel, scoop out the little grease that was there, and eat it. A week in the cooler was given to any American the Germans found giving food to the Russians. It did not stop the Americans, but when we learned how brutally the Russians were disciplined for receiving the food, Colonel Spivey ordered us to stop.

The Germans were exceedingly conscientious about protecting the Red Cross parcels belonging to the American and British prisoners. A German would be shot or, worse, sent to the Eastern Front, as quickly as a Russian if they were caught stealing any of the Red Cross food.

Packages and letters from Mary and home were now arriving more frequently. A very glamorous picture of Mary arrived, causing a lot of comments and attention. I was forced to remove it from the wall beside my bunk because the crowd of *Kriegies* that constantly gathered around to admire her made it impossible for me to get to my bunk.

Reading was limited to daylight hours because the one sixty-watt light bulb hanging from the ceiling in the middle of the combine provided insufficient light. I found for the first time in my life what a wealth of knowledge there was in biographies and spent many hours in the library.

Walking the perimeter became a favor pastime where I could be alone with my thoughts of Mary while getting exercise, as well as keeping warm. Winter came with a vengeance, and with it began the constant struggle to keep warm. The wind and cold seeped through the boards in the floor and walls of the poorly built huts. Coal was rationed to barely enough for cooking. The best deal for a *Kriegie* was his week of cooking duty. At least for an hour during the day he could keep warm. Comforters were made by sewing a German blanket together and stuffing it with newspaper, rags, or any material that gave it bulk. The POWs slept in their clothes and piled everything else they owned on top of themselves at night for warmth.

It was amazing how quickly human beings can adjust to a more primitive life style. We resorted to basic needs, where most of our waking hours were spent either thinking of or doing something about food or warmth. The survival instinct became so apparent that some even took on an animal-like mentality and appearance. They would hide food, scrounge and pick up all sorts of scraps. Many of the human qualities and mannerisms accepted as a matter of form in the civilized world were pushed aside as unimportant. The loss of one's freedom was probably the greatest cause for this depravity.

Morale was obviously the most difficult problem for the POWs. The winter of discontent, depression, bitterness, and anger would forever be remembered.

The Escape Committee seemed to have hibernated for the winter. Little activity was apparent and when asked, the reply was, "Wait for the spring. A major break is being planned." One futile attempt was made to blitz a way out one night through a short tunnel. It was started in the wall of the trench in the pit latrine, approximately thirty feet from the fence into the *Kommandantur*. A crew of six men worked feverishly all night but failed to reach the other side of the fence by morning. The stench created by the sand being dumped into the pit and agitating the human waste was so vile it could be detected as far away as the town of Sagan. It took no great amount of intelligence for the Germans to locate the tunnel, and their response was quick and decisive. Fortunately the prisoners got out of the latrine before they were discovered. The men involved had nothing to show except blistered hands, sore backs, and an aroma that stayed with them for weeks. I was not asked to join the small group led by Colonel Stillman and was glad that I wasn't.

One day while out walking, I saw two guards forcing two prisoners out of a hut at gunpoint. They were obviously on their way to the cooler. I watched Colonel Stillman stop the guards and ask them where they were taking the two men. While he talked to the Germans, he motioned to me and other *Kriegies* in the area to gather around him. Soon a large group of prisoners arrived and surrounded Stillman, the guards, and the two prisoners. The guards pointed their guns at the group and shouted for us to move away. But we stood steadfast and more men joined the group. The colonel told the two *Kriegies* in English, which the guards couldn't understand, to break and run on his command. When he gave the order the crowd parted slightly, allowing just enough space for the two prisoners to get out, then closed ranks quickly and prevented the guards from following. We all stood firm staring at the raging German guards. I looked up and saw the two would-be cooler-bound *Kriegies* run through one hut and into the next. The colonel then broke up the crowd when he was sure the two men were well hidden. The two German guards walked away looking rather puzzled and defeated. No repercussions were taken because of the incident. It was not always prudent to challenge the Germans' authority because of their uncertain reactions. It depended on the individual. Some were downright stupid and brutal. I was impressed by the quick action taken by Colonel Stillman and realized how fortunate we were to have men like him in the camp. It was a small victory but an important one, particularly for the two men involved.

Lieutenant Colonel Stillman had commanded a squadron of Martin-built B-26s in England. The Americans planned to use the aircraft as a low-level medium bomber. The B-26 was a beautifully designed aircraft, however it had a very ugly reputation. It was underpowered for its weight and wing span, and the narrow margin between cruising speed and stalling made flying the bomber rather hazardous duty. On his first mission, the colonel led twelve B-26s on a low-level mission over France. One aircraft aborted and the remaining eleven were shot down. That ended the very promising combat career of one famous West Pointer, all-American, football player called The Moose.

There were several shootings in the camp by the guards in the towers. Some of the guards were just mean and vicious, and would shoot into the camp on the slightest provocation. An American sergeant was killed in the South Compound when a shot was fired into the camp. Colonel John Stevenson was also hit in the foot when a guard shot into his hut at night. The Germans claimed that the guard saw a light through the shutters in the colonel's room and assumed that he was signaling. These incidents were reported to the Red

Cross representative but no action was ever taken against the Germans. Generally, the Americans and more so the British, Canadians, and Aussies knew just how far to push the Germans and when it was wise to back off.

Chapter 8
Senior American Officer (SAO)

Colonel Spivey, admired and liked by all the men in the camp, brought order to the camp, cleaned it up, and did everything possible to make living conditions better. He believed that regardless of how grave and dismal the outlook, one had to retain his self-respect, keep clean and occupied, and above all else stay physically and mentally active. Some men griped at the regulations, particularly the weekly inspections, that he initiated and the limited discipline he demanded. But it did not take a lot of common sense to realize that he was doing it for the good of all the POWs. His principal responsibility, as he saw it, was to see the safe return of all the American airmen to US military control. And if he had to make certain concessions to the Germans, it was done only to fulfill that responsibility and he would accept the consequences if anyone later questioned his judgement. An officer could be prosecuted after the war if his superiors believed that he did anything that might aid the enemy while he was a prisoner of war. Militarily it was the duty of every POW while he was interned to try to escape and cause as much disruption as possible to the enemy.

The colonel had the articles of the Geneva Convention, relative to the treatment of prisoners of war, posted on the wall of his room and he knew them by heart. He never hesitated to inform the Swiss delegation, on their infrequent visits to the camp, whether or not the Germans were living up to the convention rules. Through his friendship with Mr. Emil Buckmueller of the delegation, many messages were passed between Colonel Spivey and the Allied commanders. The relationship he established with the representative would be extremely helpful during the last months of the war. The slightest provocation or violation of the convention rules and the colonel would demand to see the *Kommandant* and forcefully state his objections. He usually won or at least got some concessions from the German. He found the *Kommandant* to be a reasonable man who believed conditions in the camp would be much better if permitted to do it his way. But he was required to follow the policies forced on him by the Nazi government or face drastic consequences. There was a mutual understanding and respect between the *Kommandant* and Colonel Spivey, and the latter used that relationship to his advantage. He would never collaborate with the Germans or condescend to any unreasonable demands. He just did what he considered best for the POWs. One morning I heard him across the parade ground dressing down a German officer. The POWs were forced to stand in the cold rain waiting for a German captain who arrived late to take the count at *Appell*. The colonel shouted at the German officer like a top sergeant would to a recruit and the captain just stood there and endured it. Colonel Spivey had a very commanding presence and an authority about him that even the Germans respected.

Winter dragged on with much despair and anxiety. Morale of the POWs was directly related to the progress of the war. The camp had a news team that displayed all the war news that the Germans would allow, which came from Berlin newspapers and radio. It was interpreted, analyzed, and posted in the newsroom, a small space in the theater hut. A large map with an overlay marked the progress of the front lines in the war zones according to the published German information. The little room was a very popular spot for most *Kriegies*, where considerable discussion, much speculation took place, and where numerous predictions were made. The progress up the boot of Italy by the Americans and British was very slow and disappointing, whereas the movement on the Eastern Front generated the greatest interest. The Russians were making big gains against the Germans and moving steadily west toward the POW camp at Sagan. By December 1943 the Russians had crossed the Dnieper River and were approaching the old Polish border. Places like Novgorod, Smolensk, Kiev and Karkov were common and familiar names to the *Kriegies*.

There was great enthusiasm about the Russians but little to cheer about in the movement on the other Allied fronts. Most of the prisoners thought the Russians were making the greatest contribution and they looked to them as their liberators.

Aside from the published reports authorized by the Germans, the British Broadcasting Corporation (BBC) news was available. The news came by the way of a radio receiver that was smuggled into the camp in a number of pieces, assembled to receive a broadcast, then disassembled and hidden in a hollowed-out table leg. The news was secretly transcribed each night, copied, distributed, and read to the prisoners after lockup. The *Kriegies* became quite cynical about the seemingly exaggerated successes of the Allies, and conversely, on the reluctance of the Germans to report on their losses and retreating armies. The men finally arrived at a point where Allied reports were not fully accepted until they were later confirmed by German reports. So much for the war of propaganda on both sides. We did hear, and found hard to believe, that the Eighth Air Force bomber formations were striking targets as far east as Berlin. More surprising was the fact that American P-51 Mustang fighters were escorting the American bombers to Berlin and back. Later it would be revealed that this great accomplishment, according to Göring, was a major turning point in the air war and one that would eventually defeat Germany.

An escape — the first successful one — took place in the East Camp. The Brits built an exercise horse out of wooden Canadian Red Cross crates used to ship parcels. It was built in such a way as to conceal a small *Kriegie* inside under the skirt of the wooden horse. Each day the wooden horse and man inside would be carried out to the athletic field and placed in the specific spot over a concealed trap door. While several *Kriegies* performed calisthenics on the wooden horse, the little guy slipped down into the tunnel and dug merrily away. The work took several months even though it was quite close to the fence. But the British were very methodical and careful in their effort. Some had been POWs since late 1939, so time was important, but not the most essential factor. Patience was not an American virtue; it was, however, a British one. The breakout was later called, most appropriately, the Trojan Horse escape. Four RAF officers, two Norwegians, and two Englishmen escaped and made it back through Sweden.

The great escape that ended most future attempts took place in March 1944. Three tunnels, dug in the British North Compound to insure the success of one, were named Tom, Dick, and Harry. They were very elaborately designed and constructed by the very best mining engineering in the camp. Harry, completed after eighteen months, was almost completely shored, had electric light, a track for a tramcar, and forced air ventilation. The tunnel was three hundred forty-eight feet long and thirty feet beneath the surface.

After the escape, Colonel Spivey told us that the British showed him the tunnel when he was in the North Compound, another example of the trust that developed between the English and the Americans. Spivey said it was the most amazing engineering feat he had ever seen, considering the primitive tools and equipment they had to work with, and all the more so under the such covert conditions. The German ferrets were experts in revealing escape activities.

Eighty RAF flying officers fled the night of 24/25 March 1944. The last four were caught when discovered by a German guard at the exit point of the tunnel. The others got away and dispersed in all directions. Adolf Hitler was so enraged that he initiated the highest search order in the land—some five million German military and civilians were involved. He issued further orders, over Göring's protest, to shoot all the prisoners that were recaptured. Two POWs made it back to England and twenty-four were returned to Stalag III. The massacre of fifty escapees was accomplished by a few selected Nazi—whose identities were known only to Heinrich Himmler and Hitler. The news of the drastic and bloody action taken against the POWs was deliberately spread to discourage future escapes. Warnings were posted in every hut proclaiming, "Escape is no longer a sport. Those attempting to escape will be shot." However, it did not stop later attempts. Although nothing was put in writing to stop escape attempts, senior Allied officers no longer encouraged escape activity. This action taken by them was apparently sanctioned by the unified Allied powers. By order of Hitler, the *Luftwaffe* was relieved of the responsibility for dealing with the security of Allied prisoners. Full authority was delegated to the *Gestapo*. *Kommandant Oberst von Lindeiner-Wildau* was relieved as camp commander. We were told that he died of a heart attack, but the rumor around camp was that he was shot.

Chapter 9
Block Commander

In late March, I was asked to join a cadre of thirty officers to assist in setting up a new POW compound. The Germans had completed the West Compound and were ready to accept a large a group of American Air Force officers held in a temporary camp in Frankfurt. The new camp was built between the large German military installation and the North and South Compounds. The selection of the men to form the cadre was based on their involvement in "X" activities and those who had displayed leadership qualities proved useful in setting up the new compound. Although the Germans were aware of the Americans' motive in selecting the men that would organize the new POWs, they were satisfied with the arrangement, as it would save them manpower and prevent numerous problems. I was very pleased about the assignment, as it would give me more responsibility and elevate me to a higher position in the escape organization. The move took place in the middle of April 1944.

The senior American officer of the new compound, Colonel Darr Alkire, had insisted that the Germans move the Americans out of a camp in Frankfurt. The compound there was centrally located in the city park and several POWs were killed and many injured in Allied bombing raids on the city. However, to move that many prisoners he was required to give the Germans his personal declaration that no escape attempts would be made by the Americans during their transfer to Stalag Luft III. The Germans would not move the prisoners unless the colonel agreed to this condition. They insisted that there were not sufficient *Luftwaffe* guards available to guard the POWs during the move.

Colonel Alkire was criticized by several high-ranking military men for his action. It was against the US Army military code of conduct to make such a commitment to the enemy. However, he, like Colonel Spivey, was more concerned about the safety of the POWs than he was about his own military career and said he would suffer the consequences after the war.

Two cadres of American officers, one each from the Center and South Compounds, would become part of Colonel Alkire's staff and assist him in organizing the camp and settling in the new arrivals. They would also pass on all the knowledge they had acquired from the older British and American POW, including escape activity and methods of communications between the camps, as well as with the Allied commanders in England. They also brought with them a radio which was assembled to monitor the BBC. Equally important was the "know-how" in handling the guards and other German officials. Several German guards who were friendly and helpful had passed on important bits of information to the POWs. The older prisoners knew who these guards were and how to recognize and approach the more cooperative Germans.

Within the cadre were men who were capable of setting up education and athletic programs as well as religious, crafts, and numerous other activities that would help to keep the new prisoners occupied and healthy.

I was chosen to be a block commander of hut number 165, which housed 110 officers. Under the simplified military structure of the compound, a block commander was comparable to a squadron or company commander. The block commanders were directly responsible to the senior officer for the welfare of the men under them. There was no staff or subcommanders between them and the senior officer whose staff amounted to little more than an adjutant and an advisory group of senior officers. And as such the block commanders were an essential part in the camp organization. The position required a good deal of skill and leadership.

The two small end rooms in our hut were allocated to me and my adjutant, Lieutenant Bill Munger. Two other men, Captain Jack Oliver and Lieutenant Charles "Cookie" Cook, were assigned to our rooms. Oliver in charge of a small group of enlisted men had volunteered to work in the officer's camp. These men were given a small room on the other end of our hut. Their job, under Oliver's supervision, was to receive, handle, and distribute the Red Cross parcels. Cook, the head honcho in the clothing supply store, also worked in the *Vorlager*.

Jack was a well-built young man of medium height. He obviously had been an outstanding athlete. He played third base on one of the compound's baseball teams. I don't think there were any better major leaguers that could throw a baseball across the field as hard and accurately as Ollie could. Regardless of how deep he was off third base, the ball thrown to first base never rose higher than six feet above the ground. Jack was an outstanding third baseman and a great guy, however, at times he could become sullen and difficult to approach. I'm sure it was because he was the type of person who had visions of becoming a top air force ace and was bitterly disappointed when his combat career ended after only a few missions.

Lieutenant Cook, a real wheeler and dealer, could get almost anything you wanted from either the Germans in the

Vorlager or the British in the other camps. He was an outgoing young man who never seemed to lose his sense of humor or optimism about the outcome of the war. One of his favorite hobbies was following the lives of German aces. The first page he looked at in German newspapers was the obituary column to see which one of his favorite pilots was killed or as the Germans put it, *kaput.* Some German aces had as many as three or four hundred victories. And even though they got four victories for a four-engine bomber, most of their victories were over the Russian front, so their's was a very impressive accomplishment. Ironically, the Eastern Front was where most of them met their fate.

Cookie was, comparatively speaking, an old (twenty-one years of age) *Kriegie* who knew everyone and was liked by all. He was a former RAF type who flew Spitfires in the Eagle Squadron and was shot down on his first mission the day after he transferred to the US Army Air Force. He was not at all that unhappy about it because had he still been in the RAF, his accumulating pay would have been about three times less than the monthly wages of a first lieutenant in the American Air Force.

Munger was a very intelligent, likeable young man who planned to be a lawyer after the war ended. He was married to his longtime sweetheart, Martha, who was waiting for him in Michigan. He was a pilot in one of the other squadrons in the 91st, my outfit, and was shot down on the same mission as I. He was very cooperative and willingly did anything asked of him. Bill was also completely loyal, which later would be most important and helpful for me.

Cookie and Ollie spent most of their time in the *Vorlager.* The four of us used one room for sleeping and the other as a living area. Compared to the living conditions in the Center Camp, this was a far better arrangement.

The new compound was built hurriedly under the minimum standards of the Geneva Convention. There were no double walls or floors, and the wind and rain whistled and seeped through the cracks at will. The compound, the largest of the five compounds, included sixteen huts or blocks, a shower building, a cookhouse, four large pit latrines, a laundry hut, and a separate auditorium for religious purposes or a theater. There were twelve rooms in each barrack. The large rooms could accommodate up to fifteen men. It provided somewhat more privacy than the large open bays in the Center Compound.

The area to the south of the camp was a pine forest reserve, the trees set precisely six meters apart, lined up with German precision.

My first good impression of the compound vanished quickly when I saw that it was covered with pine tree stumps. The Germans had cut down the trees, but removed only those stumps that were necessary to construct the buildings. Under the Geneva Convention, officers were not required to work. It appeared that the Germans had purposely left the stumps, knowing that the Americans would be forced to remove them if they wanted an athletic field. The decision by Colonel Alkire to disregard the military regulations was quick and easy. He told his block commanders to set up work details and remove the stumps. There was some grumbling and objections but on the whole it was accomplished without too much dissent. Removal of the stumps had to be done by hand; no tools, shovels, or picks were allowed in camp. Scoops and shovels were fashioned out of empty food cans and leverage devices improvised.

Areas for clearing were assigned and competition initiated between the blocks. Many ingenious methods surfaced and the speed in which the stumps were removed was phenomenal. By the end of May, not a stump was seen in the camp. Even the Germans were impressed.

Among the officers in the cadre from the South Camp was Captain Oscar O'Neill, the pilot I'd replaced in the 401st Bomber Squadron back in April 1943. O'Neill was a very good-looking young man. His mother came from an old Spanish Puerto Rican family and his father was Irish. Oscar inherited all their best and attractive features. He was a block commander of the hut next to mine. He had been shot down on his twenty-fourth mission, as I had, on 17 April 1943. At that time his was the closest crew in the Eighth Air Force to complete twenty-five missions and he was getting a lot of media attention. Oscar was being groomed to take his crew back to the States on a bond-selling, publicity tour. Instead Frank Morgan and the famed *Memphis Belle* crew received all the accolades and glory.

When I first met Oscar, he was one of a few men that I immediately liked. Normally, it took some time before I developed a friendly relationship with another person of my gender. And I believed he had a similar reaction toward me. We had much in common, foremost being, the two beautiful English girls hopefully waiting for us in London. A series of coincidences would follow that were destined to make our friendship very special and long-lasting.

Colonel Darr Alkire was not a large man, but his strength of character gave one the impression that he was six feet tall. I liked him at once, even though a strict ball-busting reputation preceded him. Tough but fair, and a former commander of the 100th Bomb Group, he apparently was a little too outspoken in expressing his opinion, particularly to higher-level brass. He was relieved just before the 100th was sent overseas for refusing to endanger his crews by flying them over the North Atlantic in adverse weather. His replacement, the new group commander, had earned a far worse reputation in the Eighth Air Force as being the CO of the "Bloody Hundredth." Alkire got command of another bomb group and brought it to England and a short time later was shot down leading the formation.

Two majors with whom I got to know real well were with Alkire in Frankfurt and accompanied him to our camp. They were John Egan and Dale "Bucky" Cleven who were close friends and commanders of separate squadrons in the "Bloody Hundredth" Bomb Group. They were both shot down on the Munster mission which almost wiped out the Hundredth. They had been with Colonel Alkire when he was the CO of the 100th and they worshiped the man. Egan, a block commander, shared his room with Cleven. Alkire also had his quarters in Egan's block where they could watch over him. He had a serious back injury and had to sleep on boards. Apparently when he landed his chute dragged him off a ridge causing the injury.

Johnny was a real character, great sense of humor, and exceptionally intelligent. He was slight of built and had a well-cared for walrus mustache which emphasized his beaked nose. He proudly owned a pair of magnificent, yellow pigskin gloves which he flaunted on every occasion. His wife, Dody, was a pilot flying with Jackie Cochran's WAAFs (Women's Auxiliary Air Force), ferrying high-performance combat aircraft around the country. According to Bucky she was a much better pilot than Johnny. Cleven apparently was a real hotshot pilot and was extremely upset for getting shot down. He just wanted to go on flying missions and killing Germans. If there was such a person as a war lover, he was a perfect fit. His aircraft was so badly shot up on the shuttle raid to Regensburg that every man in his crew—with good reasons—were going to bail out. He turned to his copilot and shouted, "You sit there, you son of a bitch, and take it. And that goes for the rest of you guys." They did and he got his Fortress to Africa and all the crew survived only to be shot down later.

Chapter 9

With my assignment as a block commander came considerable responsibility and a routine that kept me occupied much of the time, for which I was most grateful. The days passed quicker and with the responsibility came a challenge of leadership. It was a unique situation, handling 110 officers without any official or military authority over them. Many of the *Kriegies* in my block were of equal or greater rank, physically bigger, and most had considerably more formal education than I.

Some *Kriegies* were hard to handle, the few who didn't want to participate in any camp activities or abide by the few regulations set down by the senior officers. Inasmuch as all of us were outside of US military control there was no official way of disciplining the prisoners. True, if an officer violated or refused to follow orders, he could be court-martialed on his return to US Army control. However, the senior officers were confident that they could handle any problems and did. If called upon, there were *Kriegie* strong-arm squads that would quickly punish any wayward POW. They would drop him in the freezing fire pool and scrub him down with soap and GI brushes if he refused to take advantage of the shower program. Fortunately, I never had to resort to any of such extreme measures. I found other methods and used them ingeniously by cajoling, leading, shaming, threatening, and sometimes even begging. I worked with them, always harder and longer, and never asked anyone to do something I wouldn't do myself. The most effective way to deal with difficult ones was to give them some form of responsibility. There were all sorts of duties that could be assigned to individuals in the block and if there wasn't one set up, I'd invent one. Surprisingly, I learned that my ability to handle and lead men was a very satisfying, rewarding, and a maturing experience.

The camp leaders encouraged competition among the *Kriegies,* creating a very intense and spirited rivalry between the blocks. Saturday morning inspections, baseball, volleyball, football, calisthenics, entertainment and many other activities were organized to encourage participation to prevent idleness and depression. The most sought after recognition was a mere announcement of the winners by Colonel Alkire at *Appell.* Under the circumstances, the enthusiasm was surprisingly good and the morale of the POWs was unusually high. Block 165 was consistently among the winners and it was a pleasant and rewarding surprise for me. My block had the record for the being most consistent winner of the weekly inspections and it made me very proud.

Chapter 10

Allied Invasion

During the spring and early summer of 1944, the population of the POW camp increased immensely. Not only were the bomber crews still coming in great numbers, but now many fighter pilots were arriving in camp in significant numbers. The intensity of air war over Europe increased by a hundredfold. The fighters were now flying low-level missions, bombing and strafing anything that moved. These tactics made them much more vulnerable to enemy ground fire and resulted in many more losses. Not quite the same for those fighter jocks who were more than matching the skill of the *Luftwaffe* in air-to-air combat on bomber escort missions.

The West Compound, built for eighteen hundred prisoners, was filling up rapidly and the Germans planned to increase the capacity by using three-tiered bunks, not only in the West but in all other compounds. The number of *Kriegies* in our block would increase from one hundred ten to one hundred fifty-five. We took two more men in our two-room combine, Captain Frank Adams and Lieutenant Dixie Alexander. The former, Adams, was not too friendly—at least not towards me. I got the feeling that he resented me being of equal rank and in command of the block, so we never really hit it off and became buddies. Alexander, on the other hand, was a real character whom everyone liked. He was a former Eagle Squadron pilot and still wore the long handle-bar mustache that many RAF types fancied. His first mission after being transferred to the US Army Air Force was to fly with a group of pilots ferrying P-39s to North Africa to support the American invasion there in November 1942. Most of the aircraft ran out of fuel and were forced to land in Spain or Portugal. Dixie was fortunate—he made it to Portugal, a neutral country, and was interned in Lisbon, held there in a local jail. However, the door to his cell was not locked, although he was told to stay in his confined quarters. He didn't think they were too serious so he would walk out of his cell to visit the American consular. There, he would borrow money and take off for a night on the town. This went on for a several weeks until he tired of Lisbon's night life. He then stowed away aboard a freighter headed for England, rejoined his unit, and was shot down in May 1944.

I was receiving mail on a regular basis, and the most important were the wonderful letters from Mary full of endearing terms and the agony of being separated. Letters from home were also arriving more frequently. My mother told me how much she appreciated hearing from Mary whose letters helped to ease her anxiety and how relieved she was to get Mary's telegram. It arrived just before the one from the War Department informing her that I was Missing in Action (MIA). It was six weeks after I was shot down before they received word from the Red Cross that I was a POW.

The letters, I enjoyed most, were from Mike, short for Michelle, my favorite younger sister. I was surprised to learn from Oscar O'Neill that a good friend of his, Bill Bloodgood, was a B-17 pilot in the 91st Bomb Group and was killed a month before I joined the group. Bloodgood was from my home town and had dated Mike when they were in high school. Now, she was very much in love with a *TIME* magazine war correspondent, Bill Hipple. From her furtive remarks he was probably in the Pacific. My other younger sister, Grey, was married to

Gilbert Bundy, an artist and a contemporary of Norman Rockwell. He too, from what I gathered, was a war correspondent in the Pacific doing GI battle sketches for the cover of the Hearst's weekly, the *American Magazine*. My older sister, Ida's husband, Al Pickett, worked in army intelligence, his location was unknown and very secretive. And Andy, my older brother, who Mike loved to make little of his self-importance, was assigned to the US Army Medical Corps. She was the only one who seemed somewhat sympathetic about my predicament. Her letters were full of humor, gossip and most informative, if not a little derogatory, about family and friends who complained about the adversities, shortages, and hardships they were enduring in the US because of the war.

June 6, 1944 — At last! That magnificent day — the day which we had so long waited for — had finally arrived. The Allied invasion of German-occupied Europe. Morale jumped to its highest level. The news was immediately passed to the POWs by the Germans. The guards and camp administrators seemed as eager as the Americans to spread the news. Generally the Germans would attempt to suppress or delay the announcement of adverse news about the great armies of the Third Reich but not on this occasion. In the camp, the Germans apparently felt defeat was inevitable and preferred that the Americans and British reached them before the Russians.

It took a few days of tension before learning that the invasion was successful and that the Allies had established solid beachheads on the continent of Europe. The optimism and expectations among the POWs were difficult to control. We were confident that the Allies would advance rapidly across the continent and liberate us in a matter of weeks.

This excitement and optimism soon dampened, when after six weeks we learned that the Allies had not advanced more then five to ten miles from the coast. The Germans were resisting with remarkable tenacity and this was confirmed by incoming POWs who insisted that there was still a lot of fight in the *Wehrmacht* and the *Luftwaffe*. One newcomer in particular said, "Don't sell the Germans short, they are in this to the end." The colonel, Jack Jenkins, was the CO of the 55th Fighter Group, flying P-38 Lightnings, and was the first Eighth Air Force unit to fly over Berlin. It was the first American attempt to bomb Berlin but the bomber force aborted before reaching the target area and failed to rendezvous with waiting fighter escort. Jenkins, one of the youngest full colonels (mid-twenties) in the air force, knew by personal experience that the Germans were not ready to surrender. As group commander, he emphatically told his pilots, "Never break when you're head on with a *Luftwaffe* pilot, he'll always break first." When asked how he was shot down, he replied rather hesitantly, "The bloody German didn't break, he crashed into me and tore my right wing off."

The German newspapers published Nazi propaganda threatening the destruction of England and the Allied armies in France. Hitler claimed he was developing secret weapons that would destroy his enemies. The BBC confirmed that V-1 unmanned missiles were striking London at an alarming rate. Later we learned that a far more dangerous weapon, the V-2, a ballistic missile, was being launched against London. There was no defense against this missile that struck without warning. My fear and concern for Mary intensified wondering about her safety.

By July when movement in France and the Lowlands seemed to have stalled, expectations fell and the dreary routine of camp life continued. There was no organized escape activity in the camp. After the tragic conclusion of the British breakout in March, the senior officers broke up most of the X organization and discouraged any future attempts. My attitude had also changed toward escape since moving into the

West Compound. Although escaping and getting back to England remained my most foremost objective, the responsibility as a block commander seemed more important. Probably for the first time in my life, I truly felt a real sense of purpose and accomplishment. As an aircraft commander, I was responsible for my crew and later, as a flight leader, for six aircraft and their crews. Combat was more adventurous and exciting, and I had approached it with a different sense of duty than I now had as block commander. I had matured a great deal in the past year and had acquired a strong moral sense of responsibility toward the men in my block. My conversations with Colonel Alkire and other the senior officers also increased the importance of my commitment and my role as their leader.

Colonel Alkire despised the Germans much more so than Colonel Spivey, probably because of his experience with them at Frankfurt. After the great escape when the *Gestapo* became responsible for the security of the camp, the German officers were no longer allowed to salute in the normal military manner. They were ordered to use the Nazi greeting of raising the right hand above the head. There was considerable discussion over what the Allied response would be about returning this despicable salutation. Colonel Alkire refused to acknowledge it, which caused a bit of a flap. But he stuck by his decision.

The colonel worried a great deal about the German reaction as the war seemed inevitably to be drawing closer to the end. Would the Germans just leave the Allied prisoners in the camp and let the Russians march in peacefully and liberate us? Or would there be a bloody massacre? If the Germans left the POWs, would the senior American officers be able to keep the men together, or would the men run in all directions in a desperate attempt to get back home to their loved ones? Would the Germans separate the POWs, holding some as hostages, or would they force march them out of the camp to another location away from the advancing Russians? These concerns weighed heavily on the colonel's mind and he openly expressed his fears with his staff. The advice and guidance from Allied headquarters were not very encouraging; they seemed to say, "Prepare for the worst; just try to keep the men together and under your control and authority."

The Germans were so very unpredictable. If some of the rumors heard about the treatment of other prisoners, particularly the Jews and political enemies of the Nazis were true, what could the Americans expect? It was a very difficult situation and it troubled Colonel Alkire. The safety of the POWs and getting them to US military control without harm or loss of life was his major concern. After sharing the colonel's anxieties, I was determined to stick with him and do my part.

Summer came and warm weather brought a new feeling of optimism. Lying in the sun in a pair of shorts donated by the YMCA, I couldn't help but think that maybe one day I would look back and say to myself, *"Hell, I wouldn't mind being back there now."* Actually it was a very carefree life, if you could ignore the barbed wire, lack of freedom, and the possibility that you might not make it back alive. We had no money problems—our pay was being accumulated and there was no way to spend it.

Lieutenant Cook somehow managed to get a parole for four of us for four hours. Occasionally POWs, under escort, were allowed to venture outside of the compound, but it never entered my mine that I might be given the opportunity. It came as quite a surprise when Cookie, along with a friendly German guard named Gambits, invited Bill Munger and me to join them. The German guard took us to a beer garden. When we arrived only two elderly women were sitting in the garden, drinking something that looked like cider. One of them smiled at us. Apparently, she had not been subjected to our bombing this far to the east. Gambits bought us a beer—it was warm but amazingly good—and we thoroughly enjoyed not only the beer but the feeling of freedom. We later walked to the Bohr River and sat on the bank. There we were entertained by three German women wading in the river. There was a lot of giggling and looking but at a safe distance from us. However, the women weren't a bit shy about showing us a good portion of thigh with their skirts rolled up and tucked into their waistbands. It was a very refreshing and pleasant outing. The sweet taste of freedom ended all too soon as we treaded our way back to our barbed-wire enclosure.

At night I would lie in my bunk thinking of Mary. My thoughts about our lovemaking racked my mind and body. She had been a very passionate and unselfish lover. Such thoughts drove me to despair while filling me with an agonizing desire to be with her again. I thought about the night we met after I decided to be true to Clare. The meeting was completely unexpected and how strangely inevitable it was that we were destined to be lovers.

* * * *

It had been two weeks since that wretched morning when I left Mary's flat, bitterly ashamed of myself for not being truthful and telling her about Clare. During that time I'd been assigned to the 91st Bomb Group at Bassingbourn and flown my first mission. Feeling confident that I'd resolved my predicament over seeing Mary, I went to London with Norm Retchin and arranged to meet Sylvia, the Greek woman, at the Astor, a bottle club.

Minutes after we met Sylvia in the club lobby, I came face-to-face with Mary and her friend Dorothy who were on their way to rejoin Stephanos, Dorothy's friend, at his table. It was a surprising and extremely awkward meeting. And after a most embarrassing confrontation and the exchange of several scathing remarks we parted and went to our separate tables. Mary openly stared scornfully at me from across the dance floor. It was a very uncomfortable situation and I was completely shocked, knowing how she despised alcohol, watching her half fill a tall glass with scotch and drink a good portion of it.

After a very uncomfortable period of fifteen or twenty minutes, Mary stood and casually walked over and asked if she could join our table. I immediately stood and offered a chair for her. She began a very affable and pleasant conversation by asking me about our dog, Duke, I had inherited from a pilot who had been shot down and whose room I had been assigned. I'd mentioned the dog to her in one of our phone conversations. Then she ventured into a glowing dissertation about our relationship, audaciously implying that she and I were lovers. She had known Sylvia from a previous encounter and had every reason to dislike the woman. She apparently enjoyed watching me, as well as Sylvia, squirm.

When we met in the lobby I had implied that Sylvia was with Norm. After listening to Mary's exaggerated and shameless tales about our relationship, Sylvia, indignant and furious, left the table. Norm graciously left to take Sylvia home. He grinned at me, saying, "Bye bye, lover boy," while Mary sat there looking very smug and pleased with herself.

We then joined Dorothy and Stephanos while I tried unsuccessfully to make conversation while attempting to rationalize Mary's behavior. Dorothy and Stephanos finally excused themselves when the atmosphere at the table became uncomfortably heavy. A wall of silence settled between us for some time until Mary finally broke the stilted tension by asking me very quietly to take her home.

We arrived at Mary's flat, and again, she surprisingly asked me in. Once inside her flat she disappeared in the bathroom, returned a short time later in her nightgown, and got into bed. I sat in her lounge chair smoking and wallowing in self-pity. She watched me for several minutes and then said, "Are you coming to bed?"

I was tormented with indecision—not wanting to leave and yet knowing I should. Finally she said very quietly, "Please, Bill, come to bed and hold me." My resistance crumbled and I undressed and joined her. The moment our bodies came together, we confessed our love and true feelings toward each other. From that day forward, we became entwined in a love affair that was filled with an insatiable passion and an irrepressible need for each other. She shared my anger and grief over comrades lost, the excitement and anxieties of combat, and most of all the joy of loving and living. When I wasn't flying missions, I spent every available and precious moment with her. Her London flat became our love nest and my haven away from the war. Her unquenchable passion and unselfish love made my short stay in England the most exciting, frightening, and happiest time of my life.

Chapter 11

Summer of '44

In August 1944 a huge formation of Fortresses flew over our camp, returning from a bombing raid on an eastern German city, far beyond the range I thought possible. We all waved and shouted, making the few Germans nearby very angry. The rumbling of the tons of bombs being dropped on Berlin over sixty miles away could be heard in camp during the day and night. How the people of Berlin withstood and survived the massive and constant bombing of their city was extremely difficult to comprehend.

That summer I got my first look at a ME-262 jet aircraft. The jet streaked across the sky at an unbelievable speed. The difference in speed between that and the occasional ME-109 or FW-190 we saw was amazing. I prayed that the German effort to produce these aircraft in quantities would be "too little and too late." Any real evidence of Hitler's threat to produce new and dangerous weapons that would prolong the war was a devastating blow to our morale.

The American armed forces were not integrated and that summer the men in the West Compound were faced with an unusual racial problem. Into our camp came a black fighter pilot. He had been flying with Colonel Ben Davis's, all-black fighter group in Italy, ran out of fuel on a mission, and mistakenly landed at a German airfield. As far as the Germans were concerned, he was an officer and a pilot, and Stalag Luft III was where he belonged. His disposition was probably more perplexing to the Americans than to the Germans. The problem, however, was solved almost immediately when he arrived in camp. Colonel Alkire called for a volunteer to share a small end room with him and several officers volunteered immediately.

I did not have the opportunity to visit the other compounds as some of the senior officers had. But I had heard that everything from Shakespeare to musicals were being produced by the British POW theater group. While in the Center Camp, Colonel Spivey told us of his watching a production of *Hamlet* in the British North Compound. The play was directed by a son of one of England's most famous actresses. He said the professional direction and the acting performance produced one of the finest theatrical plays he had ever seen. The music played from an orchestra pit was so inspiring and beautiful, it was impossible to believe that you were confined behind barbed wire deep inside Germany. He said the men playing the part of women were so realistic that he could not believe a man could impersonate a woman so perfectly.

The American theater group in the West Compound put on some very good shows and had one of the finest Jazz bands around, even by American standards. One first-class show in particular, the *French Follies* produced in September 1944, was outstanding. A medley of music was put together by the director of the camp orchestra and the choreography was superbly done by a man who was a professional dancer. The YMCA provided costumes for the show through a rental agent in Berlin. The most feminine-looking men were selected for the chorus line. The showstopper was a song and dance routine done by a young man named Aubrey Stanhope. One of the numbers he sang was a sexy French song which he presented with a great deal of realism and sensuality. The *Kriegie* audience showed a great amount of will power and restraint, watching him dressed in a cancan costume, slinking up and down the aisle singing and throwing kisses to the drooling audience.

Stanhope, born of an American father and a French mother, had lived in France all his life. When the war began in 1939, he enlisted to fight for France and after that country's surrender, he went to North Africa and flew fighters for the Free French Air Force. When that action ended, he transferred to the RAF and flew Spitfires. Inasmuch as he was considered an American citizen by birth, he was then transferred to the American air forces when we entered the war. He was shot down in September 1943. He was an outstanding and very likeable young man and a great asset to our camp.

The person who I believe made the most of his time as a POW, although he isolated himself somewhat, was the naval aviator, Jimmy Dunne. Being the first American POW and the only navy officer he was given the special privilege of a small end room and he used it to his best advantage. His first roommate was an American who spoke fluent German and taught Dunne the language. When Stanhope arrived in camp he moved in with Dunne and his former roommate moved out and Dunne learned the French language under Stanhope's tutelage. Lieutenant Dunne wanted to go into the diplomatic service when he got out and believed his first step was to learn foreign languages. He moved to the West Compound with us and after an interval of six months living with Stanhope, a Spanish-speaking Mexican American, Lieutenant Ortego, arrived in camp. Stanhope moved out and Ortego moved in with Dunne. In addition to his fluency in three foreign languages, Dunne religiously read and studied all the books available on foreign affairs and the diplomatic service.

Lieutenant Dunne married before graduating from the Naval Academy and got into some difficulty but managed to get his commission and all the benefits. One of which was rather unique—each time his classmates received promotions he did too. He was shot down as a lieutenant junior grade and was liberated, not only as a an excellent linguist but a lieutenant commander. I later heard, most unfortunately, that Commander Dunne was killed shortly after returning to active duty. On his initial check ride he crashed his aircraft landing on a carrier. A heartbreaking ending to what, I'm sure, would have been a brilliant career as a naval officer and a diplomat.

Another fellow that was a great surprise to us was Lieutenant Larry Phelan. He lived in our hut and appeared to be a regular, congenial person. He was tall and lanky, not unattractive but certainly not handsome. Very much the typical Midwesterner. The Entertainment Committee solicited for singers for one of their planned productions and to our surprise, Larry volunteered. At the first rehearsal when Larry opened his mouth to sing, I along with everyone there sat stupefied. He had the most magnificent voice I had ever heard. He sang two popular songs, *Green Eyes* and *Maria Elena*. I'd never heard a better rendition of those songs by any famous American singer. The array of the talent among the officers in the POW compounds was diversified and truly outstanding. I'm sure that many of these young men that were seeking careers in the arts and entertainment fields had never envisioned becoming aerial warriors or being so instrumental in contributing so much to the morale of the downed airmen through their dismal days of confinement. It was quite apparent that some of us were not just a bunch of frivolous flyboys, the considered opinion of many people.

Women and sex, more specifically the lack of it, were constantly on the minds of most men and was undoubtedly the greatest cause for deprivation and depression among the POWs. My memories of my love affair with Mary and the insatiable passion and intensity of our lovemaking caused me many restless nights.

Much had been written concerning homosexual activities among prisoners during long confinements. The possibility of running into trouble over such activities that might occur in the camp caused grave concern among the senior leaders and chaplains. But to my knowledge—and I was in a position to know—not one single case or rumor of a homosexual act had occurred in our compound. For that matter, there was no reported activity of that kind in any of the other compounds, and there were twelve thousand male internees at Stalag Luft III. As stated by Colonel Spivey in his book *POW ODYSSEY*, "It is to the ever-lasting credit of the American officers that they were men at all times while POWs and acted in a rational manner concerning matters of sex."[1]

---

1. Colonel Delmar Spivey, *POW ODYSSEY* (Colonial Lithograph, Inc., 1984), pages 74–75.

Chapter 12
Allied Armies Advance

The Allied armies finally broke out of the beachheads in France and Holland and by the end of August, Paris was liberated. The American Seventh Army joined the French First Army and were pushing up the Rhone Valley after landing on the Mediterranean coast of France. The Russians, too, were making good progress and by late August they were at the gates of Warsaw. Rumors abounded, spread by German propaganda, that the Allies would halt their attack on Germany and join them in their struggle against Russia.

The prospects of an early liberation appeared to be close at hand. Once again it seemed certain that we would be home for Christmas of 1944. But autumn came and still the Germans resisted, and the Allied movement on all fronts slowed to an aggravating crawl. According to the German news, the Allies were meeting stiff resistance and in many areas were being pushed back by a determined and aggressive *Wehrmacht*. Published threats of new secret weapons of mass destruction were constantly being made by Hitler, and according to their news source, the V-1 and V-2 rockets were devastating England and particularly London. My thoughts were constantly of Mary and her safety, wondering if she was in danger of this new terror that rained down on London.

An astonishing stroke of good luck occurred in September when into our camp came a lieutenant colonel, a P-47 fighter pilot. His name was Eddie Szhenowski, nicknamed Schnozz, because of a striking resemblance to Jimmy Durante. Eddie was from my home town, Scarsdale, New York. He was a terrific man, a real fireball. His first words to me were, "It's great to see you, Bill. I'm going to hang around a few days and visit some of my buddies and then I'm getting the hell out of this place." I looked at him and smiled, "Good luck, Eddie." But the most amazing news he brought was that he had seen Mary in London. They met at an embassy party and when she heard that Eddie knew me she left a correspondent, the guy she was with, saying, "He was such a bloody bore," and they spent the evening talking about me and our home town. Eddie told me, "She's a beautiful gal, Bill, and she's waiting for you. You're one lucky son of a bitch." It was a wonderful bit of news to know that Mary was safe and still loved me.

American prisoners of war continued to arrive in our camp, filling it to capacity. By September the flow of *Kriegies* became spasmodic and we heard that most Americans were being sent to Stalag I at Barth in northern Germany. The destruction of Germany was so devastating that it was impossible for them to build more POW camps. The German rations were reduced to little more than potatoes, bread, synthetic jam, and unsavory margarine. The few potatoes we got were usually rotten or spoiled, but we ate them, skin and all. We never peeled the potatoes—the skin was the most nutritious part. When they ran out of potatoes, the Germans substituted kohlrabi, a hard turnip-like vegetable which was not edible regardless of what was done with it. With our crude utensils, it was impossible to cut through its coarse outer skin. Bread was one staple that we got consistently, and although it was hard, soggy, and black, we found it edible when toasted. A long line of POWS formed each morning, waiting for a turn to toast bread on the hut's only stove. Breakfast usually consisted of a slice of toasted bread with jam and a cup of instant coffee. Hot water was brought to the blocks from the cookhouse. A little *Kriegie* heater made of two dried milk cans could reheat the water to the right temperature for coffee with a few small pieces of wood or newspaper. German bread weighed five pounds a loaf and was made of unknown ingredients. Each block's bread ration of twenty loaves was loaded on a wooden bench at the cookhouse and had to be carried by two men back to their huts.

The Red Cross parcels were piling up in Swiss warehouses because the Germans couldn't transport them. Their locomotives, railroads, and highways were being destroyed by Allied warplanes. Our ration was cut to half a parcel a week. To further aggravate the situation, the Germans would open the parcels when they arrived in the *Vorlager* and punch holes in all the cans. This precaution was taken to prevent the POWs from storing food for escape or evacuation. The Gestapo order made it necessary to eat the canned food as soon as possible. Also for a period of time the Germans were collecting and counting all the empty tin cans because of the many uses devised by the POWs to make items for escape activities. The prisoners found ways to preserve the food by resealing or using outside temperatures to refrigerate the food in the cold months. They also developed a recipe for cooking an escape ration by mixing and cooking all the high-protein food with chocolate and forming it into a hard bar enough to keep a person alive for several weeks.

Each camp had a newspaper, in fact the West Compound had two, the *Kriegie Klartion* and the *Stalag Stump*. They weren't much compared to the hometown paper but they were highly competitive and served their purpose. The publications were more or less news bulletins of one or two sheets, because of the shortage of paper, and were published once a week and stuck on the wall of the newsroom. Each contained *Kriegie* art and poetry, coming production of camp shows, arrival of new musical instruments, sports equipment, information on education classes, and much more. Colonel Alkire used the *Klartion* to survey the camp on whether we should go to one-quarter or half a parcel when told the arrival of future shipments was doubtful. The consensus voted to go for half a Red Cross parcel and the colonel agreed. And it proved to be the right decision.

Christmas 1944 was very dreary and depressing, particularly after hearing of the German offensive, later called the Battle of the Bulge. German news broadcast called it a great victory and predicted that the Allies would be pushed back to the English Channel. When the BBC radio reluctantly admitted setbacks in the area of the Ardennes, spirits fell to an all-time low. The holiday week of gloom and despair ended New Year's Eve when to everyone's surprise Cookie walked into our humble quarters with a full bottle of vodka. He got it in exchange for many packs of cigarettes from a German in the *Vorlager*. Just before midnight we broke out the canned sardines and crackers along with the vodka. After a couple of drinks Cookie and Ollie decided they had had enough leaving Munger and me to finish the bottle. And that we did. With no alcohol intake since departing England, with the exception of some raisin brew we drank last New Year's, the effect was devastating. We sobered up the next morning drinking ersatz coffee with the German guards in their mess hall. Fortunately the congenial Germans escorted us back to our compound and not to the cooler. There were no repercussions and no one, including Bill and I, seemed to know how we managed to get into the military compound without suffering serious consequences.

The new year brought serious concerns and fears about the safety of the men in camp. Although the advance of the

Americans and British in the west had slackened, not so on the Eastern Front. The Russians were advancing rapidly towards Sagan. At night the sound of the heavy guns was heard in the camp. The possibility of being liberated by the Russians which at first seemed to be a very happy event, now appeared to be worrisome. There was much speculation about what the Germans would do. Three possibilities were considered: the Germans would take as many hostages as they could and leave the rest of the prisoners in the camps; shoot the Allied POWs and leave; or move the prisoners out of the camp by train or foot. Unified plans were made and coordinated between the senior Allied officers in each compound. In the case of the first situation, they would attempt to keep the remaining POWs in camp, identify it by signaling Allied aircraft, and wait until an organized evacuation was established. If the SS or Gestapo plan was to liquidate all the POWs, a mass coordinated break-out would be ordered before the Germans could act, with the hope that some POWs would make it back to Allied control areas. The commanders felt the friendly German guards would keep us advised and forewarned if such drastic action was contemplated by the Nazis. The third possibility, which was considered most likely, was that the Germans would move us out of the camp. Although it seemed impractical that the Germans would move or, for that matter, would be capable of moving over twelve thousand Allied airmen to another location. However, in the event the Germans did plan to move us, we were told to condition ourselves and be ready.

Preparations were started in December. The men were encouraged to exercise by walking the perimeter of the compounds. I had disciplined myself in not only shaving every day and showering once a week, but I had religiously made the perimeter circuit since my arrival in the camp and was now doing twenty laps, about twelve miles, a day. We were told, even though it was against German orders, to make knapsacks or bed rolls and to hoard food items that could easily be carried, and to be sure that everyone had the necessary warm clothing. Some of the German guards were sympathetic to our effort and overlooked the violations, but some of the diehard Nazi guards confiscated the food and knapsacks they found. As critical and as serious as the situation was, there was a great feeling of excitement, morale was high, and most of us felt that freedom was but a short distance away.

Chapter 13

Evacuation

All speculation and doubt came to an abrupt and dramatic end on 27 January 1945. That evening at about eleven o'clock a company of German soldiers marched into our compound and through the huts shouting, *"Roust! Alles roust!"* We were ordered to fall out and form up by blocks in thirty minutes. Initially we were given no reason for the action by the Germans, but Fischer, a friendly camp guard, told me that they planned to move the prisoners out of the camp and away from the advancing Russians.

The official German order came down thirty minutes later. The POWs would be immediately marched out of the camp. They could take nothing but their clothing and blankets. Anyone attempting to escape during the march would be shot, as well as those prisoners that could not keep up with the column of prisoners. Apparently, the Germans were eager to leave before the Russians arrived and they intended to hold on to the Allied POWs. The Russians were less than fifty kilometers from Sagan. The decision to move the POWs was a hasty one and evidently there was very little planning and preparation by the Germans.

The block commanders and staff had previously been instructed that it was essential that we keep the men together within their assigned blocks, so that all the prisoners could be accounted for. Most importantly, we were told not to try to escape. Wait until our leaders could better assess the situation and know specifically where the fighting fronts were. The chance of survival if caught between the Russian and German lines was just about nil. The Russians were more likely to shoot quicker than the Germans. The responsibility to keep the men together rested mainly with the block commanders. When we were assembled, I walked among the men in my block and repeatedly told them to stick together. It was the only possible way we would make it out alive. I was surprised and gratified with their response. No one seemed to want to take off on his own.

We stood outside for more than an hour waiting for the order to move. It was bitterly cold, the temperature was in the single digits and the wind chill made it feel much colder. The ground was covered with six to eight inches of snow, but it was a beautiful clear night with a large full moon.

Captain Oliver and his sergeants were told to go to the warehouse in the *Vorlager*. I could see and hear the activity in the North and South Camps next to ours. The POWs in the South Compound were moving out so there was no question in my mind that the evacuation was for real.

There was a great amount of commotion in the North Compound, where the British were yelling and causing the Germans a lot of problems. Shots were heard and one of the huts was set on fire. The British were apparently still angry over the killing of fifty of their comrades during the escape attempt last March, and this was a perfect time to release their frustration and anger. In comparison, the men in the West Compound were quiet and more cooperative, seemingly more concerned about moving out and getting started.

A short time after the South Compound departed, we in the West camp began to move. It was 12:30 a.m. The North Compound left three hours later, followed by the East, and then the Center Compound, the last to leave.

When we walked into the *Vorlager*, we were told to form a single line and as we passed the warehouse, Ollie and his sergeants were at the open door pitching Red Cross parcels, one to each *Kriegie* as he passed. Ollie later said that over fifty thousand food parcels were left behind, a lot of them torn open just for the cigarettes and chocolate, food that would be sorely needed in the days to come.

We left the camp in no particular order of march; some walked three or four abreast, others by twos. But the men did stay within their assigned blocks. An assortment of conveyances was used to carry their worldly goods. There were many strangely conceived sleds, and some elected to carry their possessions slung between two men on litters. Others carried their only assets in a sack tied to the end of a stick, hobo style. Most had some form of a shoulder-carrying knapsack or a simple bedroll. I had chosen to use the latter, with my clothes and food rolled up in two blankets and slung across my shoulders.

Shortly after we left the camp and to lighten our load, the parcels were opened and the less desirable ingredients discarded. Thousands of food items, dried milk and eggs, Spam and corned beef, and much more littered the side of the road. The German guards were more concerned about sorting through and picking up the food along the roadside, than guarding the POWs. They eagerly stuffed it in their knapsacks, and the older guards had trouble carrying it and keeping up with the column. It was a strange sight, this ragged and motley-looking army in all kinds of attire, along with their oddly crafted means of transport.

The West Compound moved and when later joined by the other compounds, the column stretched twenty miles in length. No one seemed to know where we were going. Most of the guards with the West Compound were strangers. No friendly guards like Fischer or Gambits were with our block, so there was very little talk or information exchanged between the men in our block and the guards. We knew that we were heading southwest, which would take us into Czechoslovakia and away from the advancing Russians. We saw German refugees fleeing from the Russians as well. It was fiercely cold and as much as I despised the Germans, one couldn't help but feel sorry for the old and the very young refugees, walking or riding on old dilapidated horse-drawn wagons with their only possessions that could be carried. They were going west as well, but using the better highways while we were kept to the back unpaved roads.

I, like most of the men, felt exhilarated and free being away from the camp and out from behind the wire. Initially, most of us thoroughly enjoyed the freedom and excitement of walking through the snow-covered fields and forest. However, being outside the protection of the prison camp brought new dangers. About three hours into the march, two fighter aircraft suddenly appeared and swooped over the column. We were walking down a narrow road bordered by drainage ditches and dense pine forest. When the planes roared down over us, we reacted normally and scattered off the road and into the woods. I dove into the drainage ditch while others headed for the woods. Hearing the rattle of machine pistols, I hurriedly got back on the road and shouted for the men to get back there with me. I didn't know whether they were friendly or enemy aircraft but they had not strafed us. The greatest danger appeared to be from the German guards who were shooting indiscriminatingly into the woods. I got all of the men back on the road and fortunately found that no one had been hit. If the planes were Allied fighters, I was relieved to know that they had somehow recognized the column for what it was. At that time Allied warplanes were shooting just about everything on the ground that moved.

Chapter 14

The Long March

As we walked through the morning and into the afternoon of the first day, tempers and dispositions changed drastically. Cursing and complaining were rampant throughout the column of men. The temperature increased a little but it began to snow again. We would walk for an hour or slightly more and rest for ten or fifteen minutes. I rarely sat down. During the rest period I'd walk the length of my spread-out block and talk to the men, encouraging them while trying to answer the hundreds of questions put to me. Some of the men were having a very difficult time keeping up. They would lie down in the snow and refuse to get up. Some developed ugly blistered feet; others were just too fatigued or weak to maintain the pace. We put the ones with problems next to the stronger and more durable *Kriegies*. I was pleasantly surprised to find the latter group willing to help the less fortunate ones. This was all the more surprising because many of these same individuals had been the most difficult and least cooperative while in camp. It seemed to me that by giving them the responsibility of caring for someone else, they rose to the occasion and willingly accepted the challenge. Some unloaded and discarded their personal items to put a comrade no longer able to walk on their sleds. Others held and supported the weaker ones to prevent them from falling out and possibly being shot.

It was a heartwarming experience, one that I would never forget.

After each break I, with the help of Bill Munger and a few other strong supporters, somehow got the men back on their feet and continued the march. Only two men out of approximately one hundred sixty were unable to make it through the first day and I managed to get them on one of the wagons carrying German equipment. The men in the West Compound came to a halt at eight o'clock that evening when Colonel Alkire demanded that the German captain in charge find shelter for the prisoners, insisting that he wouldn't go any further until his men could rest. The German said he would try and left. When he did not return in an hour, Colonel Alkire sent three members of his staff with a German escort guard to find him. They returned a short time later without the German officer, but they had found a concentration camp down the road about four kilometers which they believed would provide some shelter. The column moved on and when we reached the camp, we were told that there were only three unoccupied buildings that we could use. Without hope of finding anything better, Alkire accepted the shelter. He told the block commanders that they should rotate groups into the buildings for a period of two hours to rest and get warm.

My block was not in the first group, so I settled the men down out of the wind on the leeward side of a building where they built fires, heated water, and prepared their food. This was the first hot food or drink they had in twenty-four hours.

Our block finally entered into a building at 4:30 in the morning. There, without room to lie down, we wedged against each other and luxuriated in the comparative warmth of the unheated building. I got out of my wet socks and into clean dry ones. I was pleasantly surprised at how well my feet had held up. I found no blisters or frost bite. Not so with many of the others in our blocks as I heard several cursing and complaining about the condition of their feet. I realized now that my walking routine in camp was paying off.

At 6:00 a.m. we were told to form up and be ready to move. I asked Munger to get the men in the block together while I sought Colonel Alkire to find out what he'd planned and how much further we would walk. When I came upon the colonel, he was verbally ripping into the German officer who had deserted us last night. He told the German in no uncertain terms that he wanted absolute assurance that there would be shelter for the night before we went any further. The German insisted that there was shelter for us in the town of Muskau, just twenty-five kilometers away. He said the prisoners of the South Camp were there in a large factory. I returned to my block and found that most of the men had been assembled and the others were being rounded up. Many of the men had acquired sleds of German make and other items as well as food during their short stay. They had wandered unattended to a nearby town and apparently did a little bartering. To the German people, cigarettes and chocolate were worth their weight in gold. Even Munger found time to make a few deals. He showed me two eggs he had stashed away under his shirt and gave me a piece of fresh German bread. It was the first white bread I'd tasted in over sixteen months.

Surrounded and besieged by angry, tired, and cold *Kriegies*, shouting questions at me, I told them that we would have to walk about fifteen miles to the town of Muskau. There would be shelter and a warm place to stay and rest for a whole day. I also informed them that Colonel Alkire had told the German officer in charge that the Americans had taken control and would determine just how far they would walk each day and how often they would stop for rest breaks. He would take full responsibility for keeping the POWs together and insisted that shelter be provided at the end of each day's march.

The Long March

That seemed to satisfy the men in my block. Bill and I then got everyone together and the column moved out shortly thereafter.

Most of the prisoners seemed to have gotten their second wind after the short rest and some hot food. I felt surprising well and continued to walk among the men, talking to them during the short breaks. We arrived at Muskau about three o'clock that afternoon completely exhausted, cold and wet, as it had snowed most of the day. We were guided to an ancient brick factory. Most of the first floor was occupied by the time our block arrived in the building. The men had crowded into the entryway and collapsed, leaving no room for us. Munger and I took off on a little reconnaissance of the building and found a stairway to the upper level and discovered a large open area above the first level. The floor was covered with red dust and there were several round open holes about a foot in diameter spaced at intervals in the floor. We cautiously walked onto the floor and found that the holes were chimneys to the kiln fires below, releasing wonderful smokeless hot air. We tested the floor and found it to be sufficiently solid and reinforced. I then went below and led our block to the upper level. There was not the slightest hesitation about settling down in the thick dust that covered the floor. The heat from the huge kilns below rose like a tropical breeze to sooth our tired, aching and cold, wet bodies. We stretched out with our feet just a few inches from the openings to the furnaces below and within minutes most men were sound asleep, warm for the first time in nearly forty hours.

I had just dozed off when I was awakened by a fellow *Kriegie* saying, "Bill, you'd better take a look at Cookie. He's in bad shape." Shaking the cobwebs out of my head, I tried to understand what he was saying. Then it finally dawned on me. Cookie had cut his wrist on a broken plate before we left the West Compound. Yesterday, I had put him on one of the supply wagons because his arm had become swollen and infected and he couldn't continue walking.

I found Cook burning with fever, his arm was swollen and the gland under his arm was black. There was no question, I had to get him to a hospital. I told Cookie to hang on for a few minutes and went to find Colonel Alkire. When I found the colonel, Alkire agreed that I should get Cook to a hospital and told me to get permission from the German captain. I got hold of Sergeant Hendricks, one of Oliver's helpers who spoke fluent German, and Gambits, a friendly guard, and went to find the German officer in charge. We finally found him in the factory manager's office. Through Hendricks, I explained to the German what we planned to do. After a considerable discussion, the German finally agreed to let us go.

We took Cook out of the factory and on to a borrowed sled set off for the nearest hospital. The first one was about three kilometers from the factory but a German nurse there turned us away saying there was no room. She told us to try another hospital and explained to Gambits where it was. There, too, we were turned away and told to leave. When we finally arrived at the third, a Hungarian hospital, Cookie was in such bad shape I decided to just carry him into the hospital and leave him. We were stopped at the front desk by a matronly nun who insisted that we could not leave the American there. After a lengthy explanation and much pleading, she finally relented and agreed to accept Cook. She said there were no beds available and that there was not much they could do for him. Apparently, there were many patients in the hospital in worse condition than he. I had serious doubts about leaving Cook, but there was no alternative. When the hospital nurse placed Cookie on a gurney, I looked into his painful anxious eyes and said, "The matron promised to do what she could for you and would give you something to kill the infection. You can't continue with us in your condition. I'll try to get them to move you back to Sagan so you'll be with the guys we left there in the hospital. Okay, Cookie?"

Cook looked at me and said, "I'll be all right. Don't worry. Here, take my watch, Bill. Hold it for me until we get back to the States." He handed me his Rolex. A Swiss jeweler had graciously and trustingly responded to requests from American POWs, when they ordered watches from him. He accepted their promise to pay him when the war was over.

I took his watch and said, "Okay, Cookie. See you back in the States. You take care."

We stood and watched Cook being rolled away on the gurney. I had some agonizing thoughts about whether or not I was doing the right thing. But there was nothing else we could do. So the three of us left the hospital.

We got back to the factory after dark and I told the German officer in charge where we'd left Cook and asked him to try and get Cook back to Sagan. There were about five hundred POWs left at Stalag Luft III that were too sick to walk. They were in a *Kriegie* hospital in the *Vorlager* under the care of an English doctor. The German said he would try and I had to leave it at that.

I learned later, much later, that Cook was taken back to Sagan by truck the following day. The care he received in the Hungarian hospital was minimal, but the English doctor at Stalag III saved his arm and perhaps his life. A few days later he was liberated by the Russians and with little or no help from his host country, he and two comrades made a long and rigorous journey back through Russia to a Black Sea port. From there he was put aboard a ship to Naples, Italy, and then flown to the US where he arrived long before we did.

I was so tired when we got back to the factory that I had difficulty focusing and started to hallucinate. I knew that if I didn't lie down, I'd fall down. I thanked Sergeant Hendricks and Gambits, who were just as tired and beat as I was, and without their help getting Cook to a hospital it would've been impossible. I found Munger guarding our spot near the kiln opening and waiting to share the two eggs with me.

Chapter 15

Nuremberg

We stayed in the factory in Muskau for two nights and left the morning of 31 January for Spremberg. It was about sixteen miles and we covered the distance without too many problems. The march, under American supervision with regular scheduled rest breaks, went quite well. I felt good after two days' rest but many of my comrades were still in very bad shape, some with their feet so badly swollen and blistered that they couldn't get their shoes back on and had to wrap their feet in rags.

The snow had started to melt on the roads so the sleds became useless. We arrived in Spremberg about three o'clock in the afternoon and were taken to a military base. The magnificent facility now completely deserted had apparently once housed one of German's elite Panzer divisions now either fighting on one of the fronts or badly beaten and possibly destroyed. The sturdy, attractive-built brick buildings were spaciously located over a well-kept landscaped area.

We were marched into an empty maintenance hanger and for the first time since leaving Sagan were fed by the Germans. Although the food was just diluted barley gruel and a piece of black bread, the soup was hot and good.

Immediately after we were fed the Germans marched us to a railhead. When I saw the familiar and notorious "Forty and Eight" boxcars lined up on the siding, my heart sank. *No, not again.* I was beginning to enjoy the march now that we were setting the pace. I not only dreaded the horrible stinking accommodations in the boxcars, but the possibility of being strafed by Allied aircraft was a very serious matter. There was no marking on the boxcars to identify them as transporting POWs, as required by the Geneva Convention. Allied aircraft were having a field day strafing trains. I left our block to find Colonel Alkire in a violent argument with the German officer in charge. He was forcefully voicing the same concerns that I had about traveling in unmarked freight trains. I listened for a while and then returned to the men in my block, knowing that in the end we would be forced to board the filthy boxcars.

It was dark before all the men boarded. Forty to fifty POWs with eight guards were stuffed into each boxcar. There was no room to sit or lie down and no toilet facility. About midnight the train pulled off onto a siding and stopped. Air-raid sirens could be heard and a short time later we felt and heard the bombs falling nearby. The city being bombed could not have been more than a few miles away. Shrapnel from the antiaircraft guns pelted the roof, and some of it penetrating into the crowded boxcars resulting in a screaming reaction from unfortunate *Kriegies*. About two hours after the raid began, the train jerked into motion and moved out cautiously.

After the first night, the stench of vomit and human excrement was insufferable. There was no way to prepare food and no water. The guards weren't much better off, although they did have their canteens and some black bread. Again I was overcome with a rage that nearly consumed me. I wanted to grab a machine pistol from one of the guards and start shooting.

The following night the train stopped again on a siding where we waited while a city close by was bombed. This one, however, was not a large raid. Only several aircraft were involved. It was probably just a nuisance raid, but it was awfully close to us and scary.

The freight finally came to a halt mid-morning of the third day. We could hear the doors to the other boxcars sliding open and finally a loud rapping on our door signaling the guards inside to open up. The cold, damp air sucked into the car released the horrible stink of vomit, excrement, urine, and dirty bodies. The guards standing at the open door were pushed aside and the ungodly mass of humanity descended to the ground. We found ourselves in a large marshaling yard surrounded by hundreds of heavily armed German soldiers. The *Luftwaffe* guards were backed by Germans in black and green uniforms—the dreaded SA and SS troops. There, not only to shoot us but the *Luftwaffe* guards in front of them if they hesitated to take aggressive action on any disturbance by the Americans. The Germans were apparently expecting trouble and they were prepared for it. The anger and rage of the POWs was close to being suicidal; shouting vile curses and using the most abusive language in telling their tormentors what they thought of them. The word was passed down to the blocks from Colonel Alkire to quiet the men so they could get to their destination where they could wash and get food and water. I learned that we were at a large railroad marshaling yard in the city of Nuremberg.

I managed to get the men together and walked down the column, counting and checking the men of my block. They were all there but looked miserable, filthy, angry, and completely exhausted. When the block ahead of us moved out we followed, grumbling and bitching. We walked down a road that skirted the railyard and came to a halt about three kilometers from it. I asked Munger to walk ahead and try to find out what was going on. He came back about fifteen minutes later and said that Colonel Alkire was arguing with the German captain. Apparently, the Germans were going to put us into a deserted POW camp and the colonel refused to move the men into it because it was too close to the marshaling yard. He had lived through this in Frankfurt and he was determined not to do it again. But the German refused to budge, saying it was the only place available and the colonel could take his complaint with the Red Cross and a higher German authority. Alkire was furious but finally consented, knowing that he had to get the men under some form of shelter, fed and washed or he would lose complete control. His greatest fear since getting off the freight train was that the men in their violent and dangerous moods might attempt a mass escape. The word finally came down that we were moving into the camp, where we were promised food, water, and a place to lie down.

When we arrived, I was assigned a barracks and led the men to it. We walked into a foul-smelling, filthy building with grimy soiled palliasses spread over the floor. There were about a dozen or so bunks in a building that was divided into two large bays, room enough for about one hundred men. There was no coal for the stoves, one at each end of the building. The look of despair, anger, and disappointment was desperately etched on the men's faces. The only consolation that I could possibly find was that the accommodations were slightly better than the freight cars. Most men just collapsed on the floor or on the vermin-ridden mattresses. Others just wandered around in a bewildered state. There was no food except what the men had brought with them. I got together the few individuals whom I normally looked to for support and inventoried our resources. Some had brought with them cooking utensils and small *Kriegie* burners that were similar to Bunson burners where water could be boiled with a few scraps of paper or wood. Before long others joined in, brewing coffee and cooking what little food they had. After a small amount of nourishment, attitudes seemed to change and they were willing to listen to Munger and me tell them that if this is where we were going to stay for the next few days or possibly weeks, we would have to clean it up. After much grumbling and bitching, the majority of the men agreed. There was plenty of water and it could be heated in the mess hut and most men had soap. So this was the first major step toward improving our lot. By nightfall and lock-up, the attitude of the men had changed considerably and most were planning what would be done the following day to make the barracks more livable.

We had just settled at about eleven o'clock when the sirens started wailing. We had received no instructions or what precautions to take in the event of a raid. I opened the window and shouted across to the next hut, "What's the drill?" After several others picked up my plea, word finally came back. "Stay inside. The guards have orders to shoot anyone found outside the buildings." I walked through our block trying to assure the men that it would be all right. Most of the guys opened the shuttered windows to protect them from flying glass, what little was left in the windows, as well as to see what was going on. We watched the searchlights sweeping the sky and finally we could hear and see the flashes of antiaircraft guns. At almost the same instant we saw huge flashes from fire-bombs bursting into the city of Nuremberg, followed immediately by fierce sound of the explosions so close the concussion shook the barracks and sent the spectators at the windows back on their butts. It was all over in a matter of minutes. It seemed that the bombs began to fall almost before the antiaircraft guns started firing.

The next day we were told that the night raid on Nuremberg was made by a flight of six RAF Mosquitos. It was the practice of Bomber Command to dispatch a few fast bombers to all the large German cities that were not targeted for major bombing missions by the RAF. The terror raids intended to break the morale of the German people by keeping them out of their beds and in bomb shelters. In many cases, the sleek, fast bombers were in and out before the sirens or the antiaircraft guns fired.

At *Appell* the next morning, across the open assembly area, we could hear Colonel Alkire shouting at the German captain. He was raging mad and the captain just stood there silently looking down at his feet. Later at the block commander's meeting, the colonel told us that he had insisted that the Germans move us out of the camp and away from the city and railway yard. With the exception of a promise from the German captain to have the area military commander visit the camp and hear our complaints, he received no further satisfaction. Until then we would just have to tolerate the possibility of more bombings. The colonel stated that the Allies should know our location and hopefully avoid bombing near the camp.

Cleanup began. The barracks were swept out with the few twig brooms left behind by the former inhabitants. Hot water—and it was the only thing available from the kitchen—was hauled to our huts. The men washed their clothes and the mattress covers and then poured the leftover soapy water on the floors and scrubbed them. Most *Kriegies* began to feel like human beings again. The weather, however, wouldn't cooperate. A cold, raw rain persisted for several days and most of the men walked around wearing damp underclothes and slept on wet mattress covers. But we were clean.

The camp was bare, with insufficient bunks and absolutely no furnishings. Most men slept and sat on the floor. There was no library, no books, reading or writing material. There was no musical instruments, no athletic equipment or other items that could be used for any activity or entertainment. Our communicator did, however, managed to smuggle and bring into the camp his radio receiver. It was a most essential piece of equipment for sustaining morale by listening to the BBC and maintain a one-way contact with London. Information specifically directed to the POWs was coded and sent by the BBC during selected radio programs.

Some of the more ingenious POWs did fabricate a football and softballs out of scrounged leather, stitched, and stuffed with a mixture of sand and straw. An exercise, or chin bar, was also constructed. These items provided some diversion from the monotony of nothing to do but walk endless circuits around the perimeter. But physical exercise was limited by the meager intake of nutrition from the slim diet that barely sustained life, let alone allowed the performance of any strenuous exercise.

The promise of the arrival of Red Cross parcels failed to materialize. One meal of watery potato or barley soup and two slices of black bread was our daily ration. Some men were able to supplement this with the little food brought with them but most could not. Thanks to Munger, who had managed to hoard some instant coffee, he and I had a hot drink once or twice a day.

Five days after our arrival at the camp, the Germans could no longer provide us with potatoes or barley soup. Several days later, the Germans issued about twenty sacks of dehydrated vegetables they found in a warehouse where it had been stored, probably for years. The cooks preparing the food told the anxious *Kriegies* watching in great anticipation that it was full of weevils and worms. When it was served, most men sorted out the bugs before eating it. There were, however, some that eagerly devoured their share, shoving it down with little or no regard for the vermin floating around in the watery gruel. They then grabbed what was discarded by those that could not stomach it. They even tried to discourage the weaker ones from eating the rotten substance so they could get it.

Hunger is a powerful force and can cause some individuals to cast aside all the natural human virtues, such as self-respect and dignity. I watched these individuals and thought that the characteristics that separate men from animals become a very thin line when hunger is involved.

The bombing of Nuremberg continued and we were forced to stay in our barracks. Finally, ten days after we arrived, word was circulated that the representative of the local military command and the Red Cross representatives would visit the camp. At eleven o'clock that day, the POWs were ordered to assemble on the athletic field. We watched a German SS general step out of a staff car in the *Vorlager* and with his aide march through the double gates and into the camp. Inside he was met by the local *Luftwaffe* personnel and three civilians. They walked to the center of the field where Colonel Alkire and his staff waited. I got a good look at the general as he walked past our block, and my first impression of the German was that of a snake, a poisonous one ready to strike. The general was tall and very skinny, dressed in a green SS uniform. As he walked his body swayed slightly from side to side and with his narrow face and black, beady eyes he definitely had a reptilian appearance.

Colonel Alkire ignored and refused to return his "Heil Hitler" salute. They talked through an interpreter and it was apparent that Alkire was mad as hell with the obvious negative reaction he got from each complaint put to the German. The Red Cross representatives seemed to have even less success and were much less forceful.

The group dispersed and walked through several huts. While watching the general as he left the camp, I thought, *If Hollywood was looking for a most despicable villain-type to play the part of a hated Nazi SS officer, that man would fit the part perfectly.*

When the Germans and civilians departed the compound, the POWs were dismissed and the block commanders assembled around Colonel Alkire. He told us we would not be moved for at least two or three weeks because there was just no place to house us. The land area over which the Germans still had control had shrunk considerably with the Russians advancing from the east while the Allies were pushing eastward toward the center of Germany. There was little land area left in the *Führer's* Fatherland. The colonel said he got only one concession from the Germans: we would be allowed to dig slit trenches and use them during a bombing raid. The Germans would provide the tools and supervise the digging of the trenches by the POWs. The German general made it very clear that if it was his decision to make, he would put us all out in the center of the marshaling yard during a bombing. Nice guy.

That afternoon the shovels arrived in a horse-drawn wagon and the *Kriegies* went to work digging slit trenches between the huts. The work was completed that evening before dark, and it could not have been more timely. A massive RAF raid was made that night on Nuremberg and the trenches were immediately put to use. It was a very frightening experience and I wonder how the German people had endured such horrors night after night for so long.

When the sirens were heard, we filed out of the huts and into the trenches with our blankets. We had been briefed to use a folded blanket to protect our heads from falling shrapnel. I, like most, thought that it was probably another nuisance raid and it would be over in a matter of minutes. But not tonight. We first heard the eerie rumble of aircraft engines that grew in intensity as the bombers approached their objective. First came the Pathfinders dropping strings of flares or chandeliers to mark the area to be saturated by the bombs. It was most spectacular but a very awesome and frightening scene. The comments shouted down the line of men in the slit trenches ranged from joyful excitement to paralyzing fear. The fact that the camp was only three kilometers from the marshaling yard caused great anxiety and concern among the prisoners. I tried to convince the men in our block, as well as myself, that the RAF knew that Americans were here in the POW camp. I

Chapter 15

rationalized that we were on the safe side of the string of flares dropped to define a boundary line over which the bombs would not be dropped. That seemed to satisfy some of the men in the trench with me. But their confidence soon faded when the flares began to drift toward the camp.

The thunderous and continuous explosions were deafening beyond comprehension. The earth shook with a fury that made it impossible to stand upright. Some guys feverishly scratched and dug out cavities in the side of the trench in an attempt to bury themselves from the terror. Shrapnel fell all around us, in the trenches and onto the barracks. Shouts and screams were heard from those that were hit by the falling bits of metal. It was unquestionably the most frightening and terrifying experience I had ever been through. But I couldn't help but think that here we were now on the receiving end of this ungodly terror that we ourselves had inflicted on the helpless German people. Under the circumstances it was hard to believe that we could've been so heartless and indifferent to the suffering we caused.

The raid lasted for more than two hours but it seemed like an eternity. Before it ended the flares had drifted over and beyond our camp. Some bomb blasts were very close, but fortunately none fell in the compound.

The very next day just before noon, the air-raid sirens sounded again. A mixture of excitement and anxiety was seen on the faces of the men rushing past me to the trenches. This was going to be different. The Eighth Air Force, the American bombers who normally followed the night raids of the RAF, were on the way in a daylight raid. When in the trenches, the *Kriegies* strained to get their first glimpse of the bombers. After twenty minutes we could just hear the distant rumble of Wright Cyclone engines. Ten minutes later vapor trails were seen and finally the lead wing grew from specks to become recognizable aircraft. A roar of cheering voices rose up from the Americans on the ground as the lead wing became clearly visible. We watched with great pride as the formation of Fortresses were seen approaching us from the north. The cheers subsided as the bombers appeared to be heading straight for our camp. Someone shouted, "They know we're here!" I hoped they did. The confidence the airmen had in the American precision bombing helped to ease some of the apprehension. But not all. If a crippled Fort was in trouble and couldn't keep up with the formation, there wouldn't be a moment's hesitation on the part of the crew to salvo the bombs anywhere over Germany.

A slight change of course turned the armada of Seventeens to the east of the compound, giving vent to another round of noisy cheering. We did not see the bombs fall, but a short distance to the southeast the earth suddenly erupted in flaming explosions with smoke bellowing up above the hills. Then in little more than a minute, the shock wave roared through the compound and the earth shook with the intensity of a violent earthquake. The target could not have been more then five miles from the camp. However frightening, it was not as spectacular or as scary as the RAF night raid which lasted for nearly three hours with the continuous detonations of large bombs.

The massive explosions from the force of several hundred 500-pounders or more hitting the ground almost simultaneously appeared to be more earthshaking and devastating. We anxiously watched a couple of stragglers, apparently in trouble, fly directly over the compound. After falling behind, the planes turned and cut across to catch the formation as it turned over the target and headed westward for England. The men on the ground knew only too well what the bomber crews in the troubled aircraft might do. Fortunately the two B-17s had apparently dropped their bombs before reaching the target area and did not release them over the POW camp.

Chapter 15

The first three weeks at the Nuremberg camp passed without any supplement to the slim German rations, which got smaller each day. Red Cross parcels were promised but failed to arrived. According to the Germans, they were en route in a truck convoy coming from Geneva. Every day a large group of POWs stood or lounged near the gate waiting and watching for their arrival. Food was the only topic of conversation. *Kriegies* sat around discussing it all day and into the night, their favorite restaurants, planning menus, and making up outlandish recipes. We fantasized about our first meal and competed among one another to see who could come up with the most extravagant and succulent feast. The emphasis always seemed to be placed on the dessert, the sweeter and richer the better. Sugar, or the lack of it, became the first and most essential substance that our bodies craved. Page after page in our log books were filled with menus and recipes gathered like those of a group of women at a church social. Hunger had no rival and food became the main and only topic of conversation.

On the sixth of March the *Kriegies* heard that the convoy of trucks carrying Red Cross parcels had finally left Switzerland. The trucks arrived two days later, thirty-two days after we arrived at the deserted POW camp at Nuremberg. And what a day of rejoicing it was. The trucks were eagerly unloaded by more volunteers than they could possibly use. It was agreed that the food would go to the central mess for preparation and the cigarettes and chocolate would be rationed to each *Kriegie*. Ironically, with the arrival of the American food parcels, the Germans sent in a wagon load of potatoes, the first potatoes we had received in twenty days. The meal of corned beef hash, Spam, cocoa, and biscuits was unquestionably the finest meal ever eaten, to say nothing of the lavish enjoyment we got from the hot, instant coffee, chocolate and cigarettes, which some of the POWs hadn't had in four weeks.

I wasn't sure of my weight, as there was no way of weighing oneself, but figured I'd lost about thirty pounds since leaving Sagan. My body generated so little waste that my daily trip to the latrine became a weekly event. After the parcels arrived, food was rationed and for the most part the daily substance was adequate and most *Kriegies* were satisfied. There were, however, some individuals that lost control of their human values and continued to scrounge, steal and beg, or resort to almost any kind of deception to get more than their share of the rationed food.

News of the war and the progress of the Allied advancement was very encouraging. *Gen* was still read each day in the camp and the German news confirmed that the end was near. By the end of March the Russians had advanced to the eastern border of Germany, and in all probability had reached Stalag Luft III. I wondered whether Cookie was there and if he had been freed. The American and British armies had crossed the Rhine River and were now deep into some areas of Germany.

Back on the road to Moosburg

Stalag VII at Moosburg

Stalag VII at Moosburg

Liberation—*Kriegies* aboard a GI tank
(Colonel Bud Clark, *first row, second from left*)

GI tank completely covered by POWs

Happy liberated *Kriegies*—first happy faces in months

General George S. Patton arrives at POW compound

Delousing, and homeward bound

Welcome home

Chapter 16
On the Road Again

On the first of April rumors spread through the compound that we would be moved to another camp further to the south, and again, preparations were made for another forced march. But this time there was little or nothing to take or carry. The weather was warmer and everyone was eager to get out of the miserable camp and away from the bombing of Nuremberg.

At 1000 hours on 4 April the prisoners of the former West Compound walked out of the POW camp Stalag XIID at Nuremberg. Two hours later, the sirens sounded and shortly thereafter a large formation of American B-17s were seen turning toward Nuremberg. The long line of POWs disappeared from the road in a matter of seconds as they headed for cover into the adjacent wooded area. I looked up and watched as the formation of bombers released their deadly loads over what appeared to be the marshaling yard. The bombs fell exceedingly close to us and the horrendous impact of the bombs striking the railyards not more than a mile away was earthshaking. Fortunately, most of the *Kriegies* had moved out of the immediate area. Was it possible that the Allies knew that we had vacated the camp? Perhaps not, because we later learned that 147 Americans, along with 2,000 Russians and 40 Germans, were killed in or near the camp we had just left.

Chapter 16

It was a clear, rather warm spring day and we were in high spirits, happy to be away from the bombing and barbed wire, unaware of the loss of life during the bombing. But by mid-afternoon the temperature dropped sharply and a cold rain fell. We stopped near a small town at 2130 hours after walking about thirty-five kilometers. Once again we were told that the German captain had left in search of shelter for us. We waited in vain and remained there for the rest of the night lying along the roadside or up against trees in the cold, soaking rain.

The following morning at a meeting, Colonel Alkire told his block commanders that he and his adjutant, Major Carl Rosener, had finally found the German captain about one o'clock in the morning in a house, drinking schnapps with the owner. Rosener said the colonel was so mad he had to physically restrain him from punching the German. After a violent verbal bashing, Alkire told the German to stay away from him and out of his sight because from then on the Americans were going to organize and control the march. He would not make any concessions to the German officer that there would be no attempted escapes, but to his staff he insisted that each block commander do everything possible to prevent and discourage any attempts. He said the war was just about over and if we remained together and in some form of an organized group, we would have a much better chance of surviving. The battle lines were so fluid and dynamic that escapees could be killed from friendly fire as well as by the enemy. Further, there were a lot of diehards roaming the countryside like the SS, Gestapo, and a group of Germans that called themselves werewolves. They were anxious to kill as many Americans as they could before Germany fell.

The colonel told his staff that we were going to a camp at Moosburg, a small town near Munich, about two hundred fifty kilometers to the south. We would walk between twenty and thirty kilometers a day depending on the availability of shelter. An advanced party of approximately twenty *Kriegies* was organized and they, along with a couple of German guards, would proceed the main group by a couple of hours. Within the planned marching distance, they would locate the number of barns and outbuildings needed to shelter all the men of the former West Compound. They would then meet each block at the end of the day's march and direct them to a selected farm where they would spend the night. Again he strongly emphasized the importance of keeping everyone together. The German guards would still be with the POWs and their orders to shoot anyone trying to escape remained in effect. The colonel made a further point of telling his officers that he would personally kick the ass of any *Kriegie* that abused or harmed German civilians. He concluded by saying that most of the POWs from Stalag III were at Moosburg and he would feel much safer when we were all together. From that day forward the Americans took control and the march went extremely well. In fact, it became very pleasant. The guards seemed to accept the fact that we were in control and followed along contented to be relieved of the responsibility. There were many incidents where the *Kriegies* helped the older guards that had a difficult time keeping up, even to carrying their rifles. The weather got warmer, the length of travel was never over thirty kilometers, and at the end of each day's journey shelter was available.

The German farms usually consisted of the main house, a large barn and outbuildings that formed a square, or three sides of one, around a courtyard. Farm equipment was scattered about the yard and in the center of it was a large compost or manure pit. Most farms were large enough to accommodate more than one hundred *Kriegies* without difficulty. The German civilians and farmers were quite hospitable and accepted the intrusion of the Americans, allowing them to wander about at will. Some willingly shared their meager rations with the POWs. Barter was very prevalent and popular.

An odd twist of irony was frequently found at some of the farms. In most cases, the farmer and his sons who lived on the farm had long since been sent to fight the war. And if they had been unlucky enough to be sent to the Eastern Front, their chances of returning were practically nil. To continue to produce food for the country, the German *hausfraus* were given former Allied prisoners to help her run the farm. They were generally French or Polish and from my observation they were not only working the farm but working the *hausfrau* as well. From the way some of them treated the German women, it was apparent that they were in charge and running the farm. It was also quite obvious that they were sleeping with the farmers' wives too. I'm sure that many would probably stay on after the war and take over the farm as well as the *hausfrau* — such were the fortunes of war.

At the end of each day's hike when the men in our block arrived at their designated shelter, Munger would disappear and arrive back soon after I had settled the men with a hat full of goodies. Munger had a way with the German women, and in addition to the food he managed to scrounge, he would inevitably be invited into the farmhouse. As the leader of the group, I was also invited and happily accompanied him. On one occasion Bill and I sat in a large kitchen salivating while watching the *hausfrau* knead dough in preparation of baking bread. We were rewarded with a generous slice of hot bread when she removed it from the oven. Although Munger was never seen carrying much, he always managed to have an extra ration of instant coffee and a few cigarettes to share with the Germans in return for their hospitality. On several occasions I was asked to leave a note telling the soon-expected Americans that we were well treated by the German family. When warranted, I would accommodate them.

It was a dull rainy day on the twelfth of April when we first received the shocking news that President Delano

Roosevelt had died. We had just arrived and were settling in a barn when the announcement was made over the German radio. We paid our respect in a moment of silence to our great American leader. The Germans appeared to be as upset as the Americans, probably fearful that the new president would let the Russians overrun all of Germany. It was a very sad day, but his death would apparently have little effect on the outcome of the war.

The most agonizing and tiring aspect of my job as block commander was the constant harassment, complaints, and doubts voiced by the men in my care. I would be accosted throughout the day and night and asked the most ridiculous questions, most of which were impossible to answer. At times I felt surrounded and crushed by a group of adolescent children. They believed that I had all the answers and could solve all their problems. Finally one day, I reached my limit.

Seeing the hurt and disappointment in Colonel Alkire's face when he heard that a few of his block commanders and senior members of his staff had left the group to find a way back to freedom, I resolved to stay. Their desertion was akin to leaving a sinking ship and the colonel told his remaining staff how much he needed and depended on us. Getting back to England and Mary was constantly on my mind and as much as I wanted to, I vowed not to abandon my men or the colonel. But I just had to get away from it all, if just for a short time.

One beautiful April afternoon after a short day's march, I settled the men and decided, *I'm going to take off.* Just beyond the German farmyard there was a very green pasture sloping up to the crest of a hill where several large trees sparkled in their brand new coat of leaves. The scene was so inviting, I just knew that it was the perfect place for me. I told Munger that I just had to get away for a short while and would see him later. No one bothered to look, much less notice, as I walked out of the farmyard and up the gentle sloping hill. I reached the top

Chapter 16

about a mile from the farm and sat down with my back to one of the trees. I looked away from our encampment and over the Danube valley and beyond to the hills of the Bavarian forest. What a magnificent view, and what a wonderful feeling it was just to sit there, taking in this beautiful scene completely alone. My first thoughts were of Mary and how wonderful it would be if she were here with me to share this moment. I felt completely free for the first time in more than twenty months.

The war would soon be over and I would go back to England. Would Mary still be waiting for me? Since leaving Stalag III, three months ago, there had been no mail and before that her letters had been few and far between. I closed my eyes and could see Mary with me at some place like this in the English countryside or perhaps even Scotland. Just the two of us spread out on a blanket, a loaf of bread, cheese, and a bottle of wine. I pictured her in a beautiful floral dress of blues and greens that matched the hills and sky that surrounded me. No uniform or grubby *Kriegie* clothes for me, I would be dressed in grey flannel slacks, loafers, and a checked wool shirt.

I thought about the young German couple I'd seen two days before and how I envied them. Our column of POWs was walking along a rather deserted country road, when we heard an automobile horn and were forced to move to one side to let the vehicle go by. In the car with the top down was a young German officer and a pretty blonde girl laughing and obviously in love, and they seemed not to have a care in the world. Maybe one day Mary and I would be together like those two. With the war in Europe ending, the dream now didn't seem that remote or far away. And what of the young German couple, what kind of a future would they have with their country in ruin and soon to be defeated?

I must have dozed, for when I opened my eyes the sun had set and it was getting dark. I reluctantly rose to my feet, took one last look at the valley, the scene now fading in the

On the Road Again   161

dim light of dusk, turned and started down the hill. I ambled back toward the farm thinking how easy it would be to just walk away. Escape was no longer a challenge, it was a piece of cake. Maybe that was another reason why I headed back to the task of mothering over one hundred grown men.

Two days later the men of West Compound arrived at Moosburg, a town about forty kilometers north of Munich. It was designated Stalag VII. A POW camp built to house thirty thousand, it now had over one hundred thousand prisoners of all nationalities. Being the last group to arrive at the camp, we found accommodations practically nonexistent. Colonel Alkire had no choice but to tell his block commanders that they could no longer expect to keep the men together. Inasmuch as there was no separate housing for us, we had to try to find what space we could with former comrades or friends. The colonel gave us one last order: tell the men to hang in there to the end and stay together with the other Americans. The war would be over soon and it would be foolish to wander off and get shot. Escape was no longer a brave and daring attempt to gain freedom. It was pure stupidity. The danger of being caught up in the ground war was real and deadly. The colonel did in a sense relieve the block commanders of their responsibility and what had been a well-organized military command came to an end. However, concern about the men that I'd cared for still weighed heavily on my mind.

I went back to where the men from my block had crowded together in an area that was formerly the athletic field. I told them that they would have to find some place to bunk as there was no space available where we could all be together. "There are probably a lot of former crew members or friends that you know from your bomb groups that arrived earlier from the Center and South Camps. Find them and I'm sure they will make room for you. But above all, stay put and that means inside the barbed wire. Don't try to escape. The war is nearly over and if we stay together, we'll all go home together. You'll get shot if you try to get back through the front lines."

Reluctantly they started to disperse and all but a few soon disappeared in the great mass of humanity. For many it was like old home week, meeting former classmates and crew members. Joe and Woody found me and made room in their cramped quarters. Munger, too, was united with his crew that arrived with the Center Camp. We all crowded into the small area that my crew had commandeered. The squalid and horrible conditions we encountered at the camp were overlooked by the joy and goodwill of seeing many old friends in the first few hours after our arrival.

There were four hundred men in barracks built for one hundred. The latrines were full beyond capacity and overflowing. Tents were put up in the open area but many men were forced to sleep outside in some crudely built lean-tos. It resembled a large hobo camp, but much worse. There was no food for the new arrivals. What little food their former crew members had was shared. The line of *Kriegies* waiting to get water from one faucet circled the camp. The Americans were surrounded by thousands of prisoners: French, Poles, Russians, British, and Italians.

Frequent rumors circulated the camp that Hitler intended to use some Allied captives as hostages for better terms of surrender. It was rumored that he planned to take the British and American POWs to a redoubt area in the German Alps.

The day after we arrived at Moosburg there were unconfirmed reports that Colonel Spivey and several senior officers from Stalag III were taken from the camp and held as hostages. We later learned that they were initially taken to Berlin and from there to southern Germany. Fortunately, two friendly German guards diverted them from their intended destination to the border of Switzerland.

Many escapes were made because of these rumors. Officers posing as enlisted men got assigned to work details and simply walked away once outside the wired camp. But most prisoners stayed, on the advice of their senior officers that their chances of survival were far better. Our liberation was imminent and intervention by the Allied forces would prevent any hostage attempt by the Germans.

To celebrate my reunion with my crew, I sacrificed my wristwatch, one that was given to me by my former girlfriend, Clare, and had been worn since graduating from flying school. There was a Russian POW compound next to the American camp and Woody told me that they had lots of food, specifically, American Red Cross parcels. And that they would do just about anything for a wristwatch, even to the extent of parting with food. Woody, Joe, Bianchi, and I went to the fence between the two camps and I held up my watch. Within a matter of minutes, a large group of Russians gathered on the other side. Usually a watch traded for one parcel, but Woody told me to hold out for one and a half. The haggling lasted about five minutes and then one well-fed Russian agreed to our price. I threw my watch over the fence, the Russian picked it up, shook it, put it to his ear, looked at it carefully, and finally nodded. He rolled up the sleeve of a torn and ragged jacket and slipped the watch on his wrist along with the five others he had strapped to his forearm. I didn't think it was that much of a sacrifice when the four of us eagerly scrambled to pick up the food that was thrown over the fence to us by the Russians. Besides, I had Cookie's Rolex and that would do until I got back. We invited Munger and his crew to join us in a real *Kriegie* bash that included salmon cakes, corned beef hash, and prune whip. What a great meal it was. But within a few minutes after finishing the dessert, I rushed outside and vomited everything. My stomach had apparently shrunk and objected to the sudden intake of all that good food, particularly the rich dessert of sugar, powdered milk, and prunes, known as prune whip. I ended up with an empty stomach and no wristwatch.

Chapter 17
Liberation

Liberation! During the last week in April the exciting news of the approaching American Seventh Army made the rotten and filthy conditions of the camp bearable. The sound of shell fire was getting closer. On the twenty-eighth of April a small US Army spotter plane, a Piper Cub, flew over the camp. When he circled back, one of the guards in a Goon tower fired his machine gun at the plane. The German missed the American plane but minutes later an American Mustang, a P-51, quickly appeared over the camp. The pilot made an abrupt chandelle turn, flew back low over the shouting and waving *Kriegies*, and blasted the guard tower away with his six .50-caliber-wing guns. Nothing remained of the tower but the cut-off wooden posts that held the shed. That action scene seemed to set the stage for the oncoming assault. Just before dark tanks were seen on a hill not too far to the west of the camp. The shelling intensified during the night and by morning the sounds of small arms fire and mortars were heard coming from the direction of the town. The fighting increased to a fury, and several of us disregarded the warning to take cover and climbed onto the roofs of the huts. With a better view of the action, we kept the men on the ground informed by a continuous commentary of what was happening.

A few remaining German tanks retreated to the east but many others were abandoned or left burning. The fighting seemed to be moving directly toward the camp. Then as quickly as it started, the battle appeared to end and for a short time no shots were heard. Finally, we heard American voices shouting in the German *Vorlager*. And then, several short bursts of small arms fire were heard. Apparently, some of the German guards were holding out and were paying the price.

Suddenly, thousands of voices erupted in tumultuous shouting and cheering as the POWs watched the Nazi flag being pulled down in the German *Vorlager* and replaced with the Stars and Stripes. Minutes later an American tank drove to the fence of the American compound, stopped momentarily, then crashed through it and into the camp. The GIs riding on the tank threw rations of chocolate and cigarettes to the *Kriegies*. The shouting and cheering continued as the prisoners surrounded the tank, fighting their way to get to the troops and thank them.

Less than an hour later a bright and shiny Packard touring car, top down, drove through the front gate. The *Kriegies* quietly cleared a lane for it to the center of the compound. Unlike the dull drab army staff cars, it was elaborately decorated with spotlights, sirens, and a four-star flag flying from the front fender. There was no question about the identity of the officer when the car stopped and he stepped out and stood on the running board. The quiet was shattered by thousands of cheering *Kriegies*. Old Guts and Glory himself, General George S. Patton, stood there immaculately dressed in whipcord trousers, pink battle jacket, polished boots and silver helmet, sporting two pearl-handled pistols holstered on a magnificent buckled belt. After a roaring ovation that lasted several minutes, he climbed to the hood of the car and motioned for silence. Patton was a very impressive, tough-looking man, one who could and had scared the hell out of just about everyone he confronted. His driver handed him a bullhorn and to my surprise his voice was not deep but rather high pitched. His first words were, "Well, I guess you sons of bitches are glad to see me!" And with that another roar erupted from the POWs. After the noise died down he went on to say, "I'd like to stay with you all for a while but I've got a date with a *frau* in Munich. It's forty kilometers down the road and I've got to fight every damn inch of the way. I want to thank you flyboys for helping me kick the goddamn Kraut's ass. And I promise you that you'll all be out of here and on your way home in the next few days. God bless you and thanks again." He then jumped down and got back in the car and it drove him through a narrow lane of cheering *Kriegies* and out of the camp.

It had been a very melodramatic and emotional few hours and I thought Hollywood couldn't possibly stage a more sensational and climactic finish to a feature war film. But after all the excitement, there was a very depressing letdown. We wandered back to our hut thinking, *"We've been liberated but we're still behind barbed wire."* The word from the senior officers to stay put was passed around, but many *Kriegies* wandered off through large gaping holes in the fence.

The fences came down between the different compounds and men of different nationalities roamed through the compound congratulating one another on their freedom. Some were ugly and aggressive, and would take anything that wasn't guarded.

Late that afternoon a large fire was started in the Russian compound. Many of the prisoners, mostly Russians that got out on work parties, were left on their own when the German guards deserted them. They were left to wander through town, ransacking the homes of German families. I watched in amazement as several Russians on a stolen horse-drawn wagon entered their compound. The wagon was loaded down with furniture that had apparently been taken from German homes—only to dump the loot and set it on fire. More wagons came and everything from beds, tables and chairs, even a piano was unloaded and set on fire. Looting, vandalism, and havoc became the order of the day. The Russian prisoners that were treated so horribly by the Germans were seeking revenge and they were taking it out on the local civilians.

Colonel Alkire asked me and the remaining block commanders to help him organize the evacuation of the prisoners. The following day the evacuation began. Some left by truck but most walked to a nearby airfield that had been cleared for the first few C-47s that began arriving to evacuate the POWs. I saw Joe, Woody, and Bianchi off, who were among the first to leave. I managed to round up most of the people in my block and headed them for the airfield. The movement of POWs was slow, but it was working.

By the end of the third day after liberation, I was weary and fed up. There was more space in the huts as the men began to evacuate but the place was filthy with discarded clothing and food; there was no water to wash oneself; and the latrines had not been pumped out and were overflowing. I just had to get away from the foul, stinking, miserable surroundings. That evening Bill and I decided to go into the town and look around. On the way we passed other foreign prisoners heading back to camp loaded down with looted possessions. There appeared to be little or no effort made toward evacuating the Russian and Polish prisoners, who seemed content to stay and enjoy their new-found freedom.

The military police of the US Army was just getting organized in the area and were trying to establish some form of order. We asked a sergeant of the guard if there were any places in town to stay.

He replied, "Hell, yes—the German civilians would give anything to have American officers stay with them. You're the only guys that can stop the Russians from walking in and helping themselves to everything, including the *hausfrau*. Come along and I'll find you a place to stay."

The sergeant took us to a house in a residential area, and asked the man who opened the door if he would mind putting up a couple American officers. The German said his name was Hans Gutenheimer, smiled broadly, and welcomed us warmly in English. He said he would be happy to have us stay with his family.

The sergeant thanked him and said, "Good luck," to us and left.

Herr Gutenheimer invited us in but before he shut the door he asked, "Would it be possible for one officer to stay with our neighbors next door?"

Munger quickly agreed when he heard that they were two frightened war widows living there alone. We walked to the neighbor's house where we were greeted by two middle-aged and very grateful German women. I left Munger there and returned with Gutenheimer to his house.

The Gutenheimers lived in a two-story house with three or four bedrooms, similiar to an average middle-class American home. It was exceptionally clean, attractively furnished, comfortable with all the modern conveniences. Gutenheimer formally introduced me to the family, his wife, Helga, their ten-year-old daughter, Else, and a very attractive blonde girl in her mid-twenties, Sylvia Metzer.

Gutenheimer had spent some time in San Francisco and spoke excellent English. His wife and daughter spoke no English but were very friendly and accommodating. The blonde girl spoke English with a well-educated accent. After a short but polite conversation, Helga escorted me to the guest room. With childish joy she opened the door to a clinically clean and well-furnished bedroom that featured the most magnificent feather-down bed. The top of the bed must have been four feet off the floor. She then proudly led me down the hall and opened the door to a modern bathroom which she politely invited me to use. She left me in the bedroom and quickly returned with clean towels and soap. It amused me to see her blush and giggle when she gave me a freshly laundered night shirt. She repeatedly said, *"Bitte"* to every statement she made and I responded with, *"Danke,"* or *"vielen Dank."* She finally bowed and left me alone.

I stood there gazing at the bed longingly in anticipation of its soft, clean warmth. In the bathroom, I stripped off my clothes and then soaked in an exhilarating hot bath until I became drowsy. While drying myself on a soft thick towel, I thought what a luxury, I hadn't felt this clean in three months. I slipped into the clean, fresh-smelling nightshirt but before leaving the bathroom, I remembered my mother's words, "When you're a guest in friend's house, be sure not to leave a dirty ring in the bathtub." The tub had a well-defined ring of dirt which I willingly scrubbed away.

Back in the bedroom I dropped my dirty clothes on the chair and climbed up onto the bed. I sank into the deep comfort and pleasure of clean white sheets, covering myself in the warmth and snugness of a goose-feathered comforter. The sensation was so pleasing and sensual, and the bed felt so wonderful that my thoughts immediately turned to Mary. How wonderful it would be having her here with me to share this delightful experience and hold her close — very close.

In the morning I woke to find my clothes cleaned, pressed, and folded over the chair. How they could possibly accomplish this while I slept was a mystery to me. For breakfast I was formally served a fresh egg in an egg cup with toast and ersatz coffee.

The two middle-aged widows appeared to be quite plain and unattractive, but Munger didn't seem to mind — they treated him like a long-lost son and provided him with all the comforts of their home. Knowing that he was completely faithful to his beloved wife, Martha, I knew that Munger had no immoral intentions. He did have a way with women though, particularly older ones, bringing out the motherly instinct in them and the two war widows were no exception.

Sylvia Metzer was a refugee from Koblenz. Her parents had been bombed out of their home and she, like many other Germans, had been separated from her family and placed in homes throughout the country. She seemed quite happy and content living with the Gutenheimers, and amazingly felt no great animosity against the Americans for making her homeless. She had been enrolled in the university at Koblenz, studying to become a sculptress and was continuing her studies under a local sculptor in the Munich area. Her instruction stopped when the American army arrived.

An American captain, a transportation officer, was making a very earnest effort to become her suitor. She didn't like him, so she quickly attached herself to me and I was only too happy to accept her companionship. I told the ground officer she wasn't interested in him and to stop bothering her. The captain immediately accused me of fraternizing with the enemy and threatened to have me court-martialed. After twenty-one months as a prisoner, it felt very good to be in the presence of an attractive young woman.

Munger and I would go back to the camp each day as I had promised Colonel Alkire and oversee the evacuation of remaining POWs from the West Camp. Munger agreed to stay on with me. It wasn't that bad after finding comfortable quarters and very accommodating people in town. We would round up food left by the departing *Kriegies* and give it to our German hosts. Most appreciated was the instant coffee, powdered milk, and eggs. Spam and other canned foods that the POWs swore they would never eat again were equally and graciously accepted.

Three days after we found accommodations in town, Munger left for his home in Michigan. I stayed on trying to round up the last few *Kriegies* that seem reluctant to leave. I enjoyed the hospitality and friendliness of the Gutenheimer family and talking to him about America. I accompanied them one night to a neighbor's where several friends gathered in a musical recital. It was very pleasant and a new experience for me and surprisingly, I thoroughly enjoyed it. I was told that it was the only pleasure and enjoyment the Germans had. There was very little entertainment available to the people. Most of the cinemas were bombed out or closed, and the concert halls were silent due to the fear of nightly raids. Radio was available but used more as an instrument of propaganda than one of amusement.

On the sixth of May, I sat with the Gutenheimers listening to the prime minister of the United Kingdom, broadcasting over BBC, announcing to the world that the war in Europe was over. I should have been there with Mary, celebrating V-E Day and I felt awful not being with her. Knowing how she and millions of English people had looked forward to this day after suffering more than five long years of hardship, danger, and agony. I could well imagine the excitement and joy in London. I'll never forget the courageous English people I met during my combat tour in England. One person in particular was Mary's charwoman who typified many of the Britishers I met. Mrs. Beasley arrived one morning while I was getting ready to leave the flat. Mary had just left for work and left a note for her char's weekly visit to tidy up her flat. She insisted that I stay a moment and join her for a "cuppa" which she made before starting her chores. We sat and I asked her about her family and how she was getting on. She replied, "We're doing quite well, really. We're bombed out of our 'ome just before Christmas in 1940 by the bloody 'un. Me and my daughter Alice moved in with Abby, my sister, in her flat in Southwark. It's a bit snug but we manage quite well, better off than most poor 'uns living in the Underground. My 'arry been with Monty in North Africa for eighteen months. I 'eard their in Sicily now. I sure miss me old man but 'ell be 'ome when this bloody war's over."

Another instance came to mind. One night Mary and I were on our way home from the cinema and passed a pub that had just closed. In front of the pub a group of middle-aged women were dancing in a circle on the sidewalk, singing "Knees up Mother Brown." They were lifting their skirts, kicking up their heels, and raising their fists above their heads and shouting abusive language at Hitler, daring him to come and bomb them. Like most Londoners, particularly in the Eastend, they accepted the shortages and hardships with a cheerful, optimistic attitude and a spirited determination. London was to me the most fascinating city in the world and I loved it. The English people there were the most courteous, pleasant, and pluckiest people I'd ever encountered. They represented all the strength and determination of their great leader Prime Minister Winston Churchill. Sitting here now, I longed to be in London with Mary, but ironically I felt a certain sorrow and remorse for this German family as we listened to Churchill. I'm sure they were glad that the war was over but what a horrible future awaited them. The Germans that I had come to know, a good number of whom despised Hitler, fought bravely to the end to defend their country. I respected them and will never forget the admiration I had for the German pilots I faced in combat.

At the end of the war the POW camp at Moosburg held one of the largest concentrations of Allied prisoners of war in Germany. Some prisoners after being liberated took their vengeance out on the local people. They would rampage through town, breaking into homes and taking whatever appealed to them. Many cases of rape were reported and much looting.

Some of it was just wanton destruction of personal possessions and property, like slashing upholstered furniture and smashing jars of preserves against the wall. The Germans were helpless and the Americans had not as yet established any form of law and order. Several times while I was staying with the Gutenheimers, Russians or other foreign prisoners came to the door. They left quietly when I met them at the entryway. I would walk Sylvia into town each day to pick up the family's bread ration which was issued by the American army. It was not safe for a German girl to be out alone. She got protection and I got a lot of heckling and glowing compliments from my fellow Americans. I heard one guy say in a group we passed, "Leave it to Wheeler to find a beautiful gal as soon as he got out of the prison camp."

I enjoyed her company. She was a very personable young woman and very eager to please. After twenty-one months it was difficult, but I managed to keep my passion in check and we never reached the point of serious sex. My memories of Mary remained a formidable barrier and my conscience prevented me from indulging in an ardent affair that I might have later regretted.

I left Germany twelve days after we were liberated. All the *Kriegies* from the West Compound had been evacuated and Major Rosener, Alkire's adjutant, and I were among the last POWs from the West Camp to leave. Strangely enough, when it came my time to leave, I felt slightly melancholy and a little despondent because of my attachment to the Gutenheimer's and Sylvia, but I knew it was time to go before things became serious. After all, they were the enemy and I was eager to get back to England.

The four-hour flight from Germany to Camp Lucky Strike at LeHarve, France, was made in a packed C-47. It felt strange looking down on the countryside and not having to worry about someone shooting up at you.

Lucky Strike had been a US Army reception center large enough to accommodate two army divisions. It was a huge tent city of canvas army cots and GI field kitchens. I, along with all the released POWs, were routed through the camp for processing, which amounted to little more then being deloused, fed, and issued a clean change of GI clothes. We were given pay cards and any amount of money we wanted and to stand by for transportation to America. With the great exodus of American fighting men heading back to the States, liberated POWs rated quite low on the priority list. We were told, however, that troopships were being diverted to LeHarve and it would be just a matter of a few days before we would be loaded aboard and shipped home.

I'd just completed processing and was headed for my billet, a tent where a cot was reserved for me, when walking toward me was Oscar O'Neill. It was amazing, among the eight thousand-plus American POWs in this massive camp, he was the first person I recognized. We grabbed each other as if it had been years since we last met.

"Oscar, I thought you'd be back in London by now. What happened?" He had left Moosburg four or five days before I did.

"I stopped by Paris. My Uncle Roger is in the embassy there and he insisted on showing me the city. The invitation was hard to resist, much as I wanted to get back to London and Renee. But it was worth the stay. Paris was bursting with cheerful crowds celebrating the end of the war."

"Well, it's great seeing you, Oscar. Have you been processed yet? There's really not a hell of a lot to it. I'm ready to leave."

"I just arrived. Show me what I have to do and we'll take off in the morning for Paris. I checked the flights out of LeBourget and we shouldn't have any trouble getting a flight to London."

"Well, Oscar, I followed you to Germany and it looks like I'm destined to follow you back to London."

Chapter 18

Reunited

The following morning Oscar and I hitched a ride to Paris in a weapons carrier and the driver, an American sergeant, graciously dropped us off at LeBourget. That afternoon we crowded aboard a C-47 and flew to Northolt, an RAF airfield near London.

It was late afternoon by the time we arrived to our assigned billets at the Lincoln House in Knightsbridge. We stopped on the way at the army finance office to get an advance of a hundred pounds sterling on back pay due us. After checking into the hotel, we immediately got on separate phones. I dialed the number that I knew so well, somewhat shaky, I must admit. After six or seven rings, I hung up the phone and turned to see how Oscar had made out. He was gone. Apparently he successfully got through to his girl. I walked into a bar by the hotel lobby, had a drink, and called her again. Still no answer. I went to my room to shower, change into a clean shirt and shorts, and redialed Mary once more. Still no reply and I wondered whether something had happened to her. I hadn't heard from Mary in over five months and I became quite concerned. The German V-1 and V-2 bombs had caused considerable damage and many casualties in London during the last months of the war. After an agonizing period of indecision, I decided to go to the Astor, a bottle club

Chapter 18

where I first met Mary. Apart from Mary's flat, it was the only place that came to mind. I guess I should have gotten a cab to Ivor Court and waited on her doorstep. But I didn't.

I was immediately recognized and welcomed by the club manager and presented with a bottle of Teachers. The warm reception helped to elevate my spirits, but as I sat at the bar sipping scotch and watching the activity in the club, my mind was filled with memories of Mary. It was ten o'clock and after one drink I decided to call her one more time.

After two short rings, "Hullo?"

Stunned momentarily by hearing that wonderful familiar voice, I finally responded with, "Hi. It's Bill."

A silence that seemed to last forever followed, and then, "Bill who?"

"Bill Wheeler. Who do you think?"

Followed almost immediately by Mary's cool response, "Where are you?" When I told her she replied sharply, "What are you doing there? You come straight home. Right now!" And before I had a chance to reply there was an abrupt disconnect.

I stood there for several minutes holding the silent receiver and said aloud, "Damn. What kind of a welcome back was that? It sure didn't sound like she was expecting me."

I left the club and took a cab to Ivor Court. In the lobby I rang Mary's flat and the buzzer immediately released the door lock. I walked down the hall and just before I reached her door it opened and there she stood, as beautiful as I had pictured her so many, many times in my mind. She was dressed in a full length white silk slip. Apparently I'd caught her before she finished dressing. I was speechless.

Her first words were completely unexpected, "Why did you leave me the way you did nearly two years ago?" She stopped, looked at me closely, and then said, "What are you standing out there for? Come in and kiss me."

I did, rather awkwardly, take her in my arms and kiss her. When I released her, she looked up at me and said, "Oh, my darling. What have they done to you? You've lost so much weight. You look awful."

"Oh, I'm fine. I feel great."

"Well, you don't look that great. What were you doing at the Astor?"

"Waiting for you to get home. I've been calling you since six o'clock."

"Well, I went out to dinner and then to a film. You could have let me know you were coming."

I let that pass and said, "Well, I'm here now. Let's go back to the Astor. I left nearly a full bottle of scotch there."

Mary finished dressing and we found a cab and went back to the Astor. Most patrons there were still celebrating the Allied victory in Europe. Some of them looked like they had been at it since V-E Day, a week ago. Initially I accepted the cheerful crowd toasting and congratulating each other. But after watching the people, many of whom were civilians, my attitude changed. Mary had mentioned that many of them had bought their way out of military service and made huge profits as civilians on the war. Before long I became sullen and annoyed watching the celebrants. I reached a point where I felt a greater respect for the Germans. When Mary realized that I was getting annoyed, she said, "Let's go home, Bill. You don't look like you are enjoying this very much."

"Okay, I'm ready. It seems so hypocritical the way some of these people are acting. Those who did so little to win the war were cheering the loudest, and the ones that suffered the most and fought the hardest were not here to celebrate. It makes such a mockery of the victory and the whole bloody war."

My bad mood didn't change on the way back and remained even after we arrived at Mary's flat. My sudden gift of freedom, although overwhelming, had certain drawbacks.

Chapter 18

Being thrust back into a civilized world without the benefit of counsel or preparation was somewhat disconcerting and frustrating. At Camp Lucky Strike, the ex-POWs were deloused, fed, given a clean change of clothes, and dismissed. That was the extent of reconditioning we got in preparing us to return to a cultured society and a civilized world. There was also an unsettling void in the pit of my stomach. I was no longer responsible for all those men whom I had fathered and cared for as a block commander. I was released from the responsibility as well as the confinement, and I should be happy and exhilarated. I was back in London, the city I loved, and reunited with Mary, the woman I loved. How many countless times while in Germany did I dream of this moment? But when we first met a few hours ago, both of us were a little reticent and withdrawn. Mary greeted me like an old friend she hadn't seen for some time. It was a very casual and seemingly unenthusiastic reception. Was it my imagination or was I just looking for something wrong to satisfy my own self-pity? My unusual and angry reaction to the people I'd seen at the Astor was not characteristic. Was I resentful, or was my sympathy for the Germans wrong and was it affecting my feelings toward the English and possibly Mary as well? And what about my feelings toward Mary? Had I changed or had she? Perhaps it was the scotch. I had several drinks and maybe after twenty months of sobriety, I just couldn't handle that amount of whiskey without some disagreeable reaction.

Mary too seemed troubled about something. She certainly wasn't the vivacious outgoing person I remembered. Maybe she had met someone else and she wasn't sure whether or not she still loved me. After Mary's many questions and my rather short and abrupt answers our conversation seemed to be going nowhere. She finally suggested that we retire as she had a work day tomorrow. We undressed and got in bed. Our first embrace was rather clumsy and hesitant. But we came together and made love quickly. Neither she nor I seemed eager or had the inclination to continue our sexual reunion and so we both fell off in a troubled sleep. The dreams I nurtured during my long confinement of the wonderful sex we had so lovingly enjoyed together now was far short of my expectations.

The following morning, Tuesday, I was awakened by a whistling kettle.

"I'm sorry I woke you. You were sleeping so soundly. But I must leave." I rubbed my eyes, sat up, and yawned, feeling somewhat perplexed and unsure of where I was. I first saw the sunlit windows and then turned toward her voice. Mary, dressed, was standing in the alcove by her little stove.

"Hi. Where are you going?"

"To work. Tea? Would you like a cup of tea?"

She poured a cup of tea and handed it to me and sat down in her lounge chair. She drank her tea silently while watching me curiously.

I held her eyes for a moment then glanced down and sipped my tea, looked back up at her and said, "Do you have to go to work today?"

"I'm afraid so. Mr. Chalmers has some buyers coming in this morning and I must be there to model his coats." She hesitated for a moment. "While I'm at work why don't you check out of your hotel? I'll meet you and your friend for lunch. Is that all right?" I had previously told her that I agreed to meet Oscar at noon at the Deanery, a small club off Park Lane.

"Fine."

She set her teacup down, walked over, bent down, and kissed me. "Bye. See you at twelve. There's not much here to eat. Why don't you have breakfast at Lyons on the corner of Baker Street and Marylebone? I'll shop for food after work."

"Can't you wait a few minutes while I dress and we'll have breakfast together."

Chapter 18

"I'm sorry, Bill, I can't. I'm late now so I must hurry," and she left.

I got up, found an old toothbrush of mine, shaved with Mary's razor, washed and dressed. Just before leaving her flat I noticed a letter on the mantel shelf. I looked at Mary's familiar handwriting and pick up the unsealed envelope and saw that it was addressed to Lieutenant Hal McMillan. I put the letter back on the shelf and turned to leave but my curiosity overcame any scruples I may have had and picked up the envelope again. I opened it and the first sentence stopped me cold. I quickly replaced the letter in the envelope and put it back on the mantel. The letter started with the phrase, "It would be so wonderful if you were here and we could cuddle up . . ." I was stunned. Angry and a jealous rage tore through me. My mind clouded with ugly thoughts and resentment and my first impulse was to take off. Get away. But finally I grudgingly shook off the terrible feeling of betrayal, left her flat, and walked to Lyons Corner House. Over bangers, chips, and coffee, I tried to rationalize my initial reaction. There was someone else! That's why she was so distant and reticent last night. So unlike the Mary I remember. Then again, maybe it not a serious affair and I'm jumping to unjust conclusions. On the other hand did I truly expect Mary to be faithful to me when I told her numerous times not to wait and to find someone else. My letters never really promised any sort of a life together. She had every right to date and meet people. Mary loved people and she had to be around them. Besides I had a little fling with Sylvia and that happened within a week after my release from POW camp. I didn't wait twenty-one months in London.

I left the restaurant and crossed over Marylebone Road to Gloucester Place. It was a beautiful mild May day and I wandered along the familiar road, seeing all the buildings and shops that I remembered. At Oxford Street I turned toward Marble Arch, crossed over to Bayswater Road and walked beside the park entering it at Victoria Gate. I unconsciously followed the same path that Mary and I had walked our first Sunday together. Two years ago—it seemed such a long time. I remembered how wonderful I felt and how fascinating she was, so vibrant and animated in describing London's famous sites as we walked through the park. It was before we had made love physically and before my combat tour began. It was the beginning of the most sensual and exciting time of my life. So much had happened since then and as I traced our path through the park, I was again overcome with a feeling of desolation and loneliness, and many confused thoughts crossed my mind. *Why now did we seem so strange towards each other? Was it me? Or had Mary changed and found someone else?*

I came out of the park at the Edinburgh Gate, crossed over to Knightsbridge, and turned up Brompton Road towards Harrods. I passed the famous store and stopped to look into the small tea shop where Mary and I had spent that promising Sunday afternoon. Seeing it reminded me of how enjoyable and wonderful it was. That seemed to wash away some of the doubts and helped to bring back that deep affection and desire I felt for Mary. I finally snapped out of my daydreaming and realized that I had to backtrack to get to my hotel on Basil Street. I checked out of the Lincoln House, picked up my meager belongings, hailed a taxi, and reached the Deanery just as Oscar and a beautiful brunette arrived. Oscar introduced me to Renee. She was a former London showgirl and she was stunning. They certainly were a handsome couple.

After the introduction, Oscar asked, "Is Mary joining us?"

"Yes. She should be along any minute now," I replied.

"Great. Let's have a drink while we're waiting."

We went into the club and up to the small bar which could seat no more than three couples. Mary came in just as the drinks were served. She smiled at Renee, said hello, and shook Oscar's hand when I introduced him. When offered a drink, she declined

Chapter 18

saying it was much too early for her. Mary knew Renee's sister, Ann Taylor, whom she had met while doing film work. Ann was now London's most celebrated musical comedy star.

When we were all seated, Renee held up her glass and said, "Oscar and I are getting married."

Mary's face mirrored surprise, but she recovered quickly and said, "How wonderful. Congratulations!"

I turned to Oscar and said, "Great. Congratulations! But what about the three-month waiting period?"

Oscar grinned, "I'm sure they'll overlook that because we were POWs. I'm going to the embassy to see the American consul to get permission to marry Renee. He's a friend of my dad's. Would you like to come along?"

It was very sudden and I wasn't quite prepared for such an impulsive move. We had not talked about marriage in the little time we had been together. I looked at Mary and she met my eyes searching for some sign and her reaction surprised me when she said, "Why don't you go along with Oscar, Bill."

I replied rather hesitantly, "Okay."

We finished our drinks and as Oscar and I stood to leave, Renee said, "We'll wait here and have lunch when you return. Hurry back." She then turned to the bartender and ordered another drink. When Renee noticed Mary's surprised reaction she laughed and said, "Come on, Mary, have a go, this calls for a celebration. Oscar and Bill are back and we're going to be married."

"No, thank you, Renee, I think I'll wait until they get back."

Walking down Upper Grosvenor Street, I was still a quite uncertain by this sudden turn of events. I really hadn't thought about asking her, and although I loved her and wanted to be with her, I wasn't quite sure. Marriage was a pretty serious step. . . was I ready for it? She must still love me? She urged me to go with Oscar. But I wondered, remembering last night, the strange awkwardness that seemed to come between us.

Besides I hadn't formally proposed to her and it just didn't seem right saying, "Okay, Oscar, I'll go along with you."

But I did and when we got to the American embassy, it looked like I'd get a reprieve. A line of American GIs and English girls, some with children, stretched out, around the embassy and back up North Audley Street. I grabbed Oscar's arm and said, "No way am I going to get in that line."

"Me neither. Follow me," he replied. We walked up to the front entrance past all the staring faces and when the Marine guard stopped us, Oscar said, "I have an appointment with Mr. Seymour, the consul general. Would you mind calling up and telling him that Captain O'Neill is here to see him."

The Marine picked up the house phone and after a very short conversation, hung up, stepped aside, and said, "Take the stairway to the right, sir, his office is on the first floor down the end of the middle corridor."

"Oscar, are you sure you know what you're doing? That crowd out there will mob us if they know we're getting in ahead of them," I offered defensively.

"Don't worry, Bill, it will only take a few minutes. Besides I've been waiting two years. A hell of a lot longer than any of them. So let's go."

We were ushered right into the consular's office by the receptionist. A good-looking, tall, grey-haired man dressed in a dark suit stood from behind his desk, stepped forward, and held out his hand. "Well, Captain O'Neill, I'm pleased to meet you. I've heard a lot about you. Welcome back. I understand you want to get married?

"Yes sir, I do. This is Captain Bill Wheeler, sir, and he too would like to get your permission. We'd like to get married as soon as possible."

I shook the gentleman's hand and said, "I'm pleased to meet you, Mr. Seymour." And added not too forcefully, "Yes sir, I would like to get permission as well."

"Well, I think I can manage that. The cooling-off period as you know is three months. But if you still want to get married after two years, I'm sure you both have thought it over very carefully." Then jokingly, "But for the life of me, I can't understand how you two young men, after being incarcerated in a prison camp, want to jump right back into one of marriage." He laughed heartily and then added, "Well, no matter. You both look like intelligent young men and I'm sure you know what you're doing." He held out his hand and congratulated Oscar and me. He then reached over to his desk, picked up two form letters, and signed them, saying, "Just fill in the blanks and you'll be all set. Good luck and may both your marriages be a long and happy confinement."

We shook hands once again and thanked him profusely and left when he mentioned the number of couples waiting outside.

On our way back to the restaurant, l was still not that confident and positive about what I was about to do. But in all honestly I felt rather strangely excited and asked Oscar, "When do you and Renee plan to get married?"

"Saturday. How about you?"

"Saturday? So soon." I thought about it for several minutes and then said, "Well, it's okay with me if Mary agrees."

When we got back to the Deanery and I told Mary, she smiled broadly, came over, reached up and kissed me and locked her arm in mine. She did look happy and that made me feel better.

We had one more drink to seal our wedding agreements. Mary joined the toast by drinking a glass of white wine. We then indulged ourselves in a marvelous lunch of grilled chicken breast in a lemon sauce complemented with a bottle of Graves. It was an excellent and delicious meal and it suddenly occurred to me that it was the first good food I had eaten in nearly two years.

With the exception of Renee, there was very little animated conversation over our forthcoming marriages. She apparently had the full support of her family and had started making elaborate plans for her wedding. Whereas Oscar, on several occasions during lunch, mentioned his concern over his family's reaction to his marriage. He hadn't told them and apparently they knew very little about Renee. He didn't expect any of his family to attend their wedding. His family lived in Rio de Janeiro. He said with some nervousness, "I have to wire my mother and father this afternoon. I know they're going to be surprised. Really surprised."

Mary also appeared happy but had very little to say. I assumed she was worried about her mother's reaction and what if any support she could expect from her family. I also felt sure she was still troubled about my seemingly lack of enthusiasm. And was seriously wondering whether we were rushing into something that we weren't ready for.

Sounding somewhat enthusiastic, I added, "Yes, I better get a telegram off to my folks. My brother Andy is in England. I'll give him a call as well." But for the most part I remained quiet and rather pensive. Fortunately, Renee's enthusiasm and lively chatter monopolized the conversation and hid both Mary's and my anxiety and unresponsiveness.

After leaving Oscar and Renee, I hailed a taxi to take Mary back to work. Neither of us spoke for some time and finally Mary said, "Bill, why are you so quiet? You seem uncertain and not too happy about getting married. I know it's all happened very suddenly, but I don't want you to feel that you're being rushed into something that you're not ready for. Please tell me honestly that you truly love me and want to marry me. I won't go through with it unless I know in my heart that you do love and want me."

I took her hand, turned, and looked into those beautiful, magnificent green eyes and replied, "Mary, I do love you and

I want to marry you. Please believe me. It's just that it has happened so fast, I can't believe that we're really getting married. Just give me a little time to adjust to the idea and everything will be fine. I'll drop you off and pick you up later. What do you think Mr. Chalmers' reaction will be? Do you think he might want you to continue working until he can find someone to replace you?"

Mary said, "I don't anticipate any problem with Mr. Chalmers. But I must be certain, Bill, that you want to go through with the wedding. I don't want to quit my job if we decide not to get married."

"Yes, babe, I'm sure." I kissed her but then she drew back and looked into my eyes, in search for some positive sign. I held her eyes unflinchingly but she still appeared uncertain and skeptical.

"Mary, please, believe me. We're going to get married this Saturday, so tell Mr. Chalmers."

"All right, Bill. I'll tell him. What do you plan to do this afternoon?"

"I have some shopping to do. I need some shirts, underwear, and socks and most of all a decent pair of shoes. I can get most of it at the Base Exchange. I'd also like to find a better-fitting uniform. Where should I look for one? Wasn't there a men's store near the Jules Club?"

"Yes. That's Simpsons. You might try Geives and Fawkes on Savile Row. They specialize in military uniforms. It's not that far from Grosvenor Square."

"Okay. I'll call you when I finish. Let me know what time to pick you up." The taxi let us off at Oxford Circus and I walked Mary to the entrance leading up to Mr. Chalmers' business.

"Goodbye, darling, call me." She searched in her bag for a card and said, "Here's Mr. Chalmers' number. I'm sure he'll let me leave early. We'll shop for food on the way home. I've been saving my ration coupons just for this occasion."

"Okay. Bye, Mary. I'll come up and say hello to Mr. Chalmers when I stop by for you."

We kissed and she hurried up the stairs.

Chapter 19

Marry Me

I wasn't very successful in finding a decent uniform as most were made-to-order. There was a brown British army uniform that fit me and I thought about buying that. The air force was pretty liberal about wearing uniforms that weren't standard issue. But I decided to wait and see what Mary thought about it. Now that I was getting married I thought, *better clear it with my wife first* – that reaction certainly surprised me. But I had to do something about the GI uniform issued to me at Lucky Strike, which was too large and felt like a sack. However, I did get all the essentials at the Base Exchange on the corner of North Audley Street and Grosvenor Square and called Mary when I finished.

It was four o'clock when I got to Chalmers' shop. He welcomed me and graciously released Mary from her job that afternoon and gave her a bonus of a month's salary. He shook my hand warmly and said, "Congratulations. You're a very lucky bloke. You'll take good care of our Mary because she's a very special young woman. We love her and will miss her very much."

I thanked him and promised him that I'd take good care of Mary.

On the way to Mary's flat, we stopped at the green grocer on Ivor Place around the corner from her flat. She was ecstatic and flushed with excitement, buying more food than she ever dreamed possible. At the fish monger she bought, what I believed to be a large flounder, but she insisted that it was plaice. I wasn't particularly fond of fish, but said nothing for fear of spoiling Mary's enthusiasm over her extravagant shopping spree and her eagerness to cook me a fine dinner.

The sauteed fish she prepared would forever be the best I'd ever tasted. After several scotches and a bottle of excellent white wine, my mood mellowed and eagerly told Mary how much she would like my family and America.

After dinner we sat together on Mary's daybed drinking coffee. She took a deep breath and started to speak. "We were both very impulsive today about getting married. Probably caught up in the enthusiasm being with Oscar and Renee. But before we go through with it, I want to tell you something that you should know before we get married. She stopped for a moment, then continued rather hesitantly, "You know I dated while you were in Germany." She looked at me guardedly for some reaction.

When I said nothing she began again, "For the first several months I felt so horrible — completely devastated. I missed you so much. The thought of being with anyone else was unthinkable. I was very lonely and after several months with Dorothy's encouragement I started going out. It was just a matter of getting out, meeting people, and enjoying their company. You know how much it means to me to be with people. I just couldn't shut myself off from everyone. I was very open and truthful about my relationship with you and it was more or less accepted by the men I dated and those that didn't accept it never called again."

"I know, Mary, I encouraged you in my letters and I certainly didn't expect you to be a hermit and lock yourself in your flat until I got back." I responded truthfully.

"I hadn't heard from you in over five months and your letters before that weren't very endearing and you never mentioned marriage. Serious questions plagued me and I began to believe that you no longer loved me. Thinking that you would not come back to England but go directly to America and to that other woman. I forgot her name.

"Several months ago I met a lieutenant, Hal McMillan. In some respects he reminded me of you. He was a navigator on General Spaatz's personal aircraft and not a member of a combat aircrew. He drank very little, didn't smoke. Well . . . perhaps not exactly like you in that respect."

I started to respond but remained quiet and waited for her to continue. I glanced over to the mantle shelf and saw that the envelope was not there.

"He was a real fine person, attractive, well mannered, and very considerate. I told him about you but he persisted on calling me and we began to date. He was a good dancer and when he was in town we would have dinner at a restaurant where there was music. I enjoyed being with him and...and to be perfectly honest I liked him very much and if it hadn't been for you, I might very well have fallen in love with him. He told me he loved me very much and that he wanted to marry me. He was a real decent fellow, quite innocent really. He never forced himself on me in any way. I'm sure he'll make some lucky girl a perfect husband.

"Three months ago I came down with the measles and was confined to my flat for ten days. Mr. Chalmers and his wife, Paula, as well as Dorothy came to see me. Hal told me he'd had measles so I wouldn't worry about him catching the disease. He came to see me almost every day while I was sick. As the general's navigator he had access to their mess and the food he brought and prepared for me was unbelievable. He was wonderful and would sit with me for hours. The general's plane was kept at Northholt and when he was in London, Hal was free to come by just about every day. He was very good to me and I became very fond of him. And that's about it. I should have told you about him last night."

"Were you out with him last night?" I asked.

"No. I went to dinner and a film with Benny Newman. We saw the *Gay Caboleros* I think I told you about him. He's a friend of Mr. Chalmers. In fact, he helped me get my job there. He's a Jewish man, not very attractive but very generous and pleasant and he's been very good to me. He enjoys taking me out particularly when we're seen by his friends. I don't mean to sound egotistical but he does like to be seen with me, and I like him, enjoy being with him, especially when he takes me to dinner. You know how I love to eat. I'd never refuse a free meal. He treats me like a friend and has never made any indecent advances. He is a gentleman in that respect."

"Do you plan to see this guy, McMillan, again?"

"No, Bill, I won't see him again. I'll write and tell him that you're back and we're going to get married. He's in America now with the general's plane. I know he will be very upset but I told him if you came back and wanted to marry me, I would. If I married anyone else it would be wrong—horribly wrong—and I'd regret it all my life.

"You know, Bill, last night was far from the happy and affectionate reunion I'd dreamed about. You seemed different and strange and that was not the way I remembered you. The way you reacted to those people at the Astor surprised me. You probably more than anyone there had greater reason to celebrate yet you became belligerent and resentful. You were cold and distant and not once did you tell me how much you missed or loved me. And I wondered whether you still did.

"I'd heard the American POWs were released two weeks ago and when I didn't hear from you, I was afraid you weren't coming back to me. I thought you would try to contact me and let me know you were safe. I was troubled and it probably showed when I first saw you standing there at my door last night. I should have been more enthusiastic and affectionate but for some reason I felt restrained. We weren't very loving towards each other last night. Perhaps it was my fault—we were like strangers. When I left you this morning, I wasn't at all sure that you still loved me. It was very disturbing and strange."

"I probably overreacted and was disappointed when you didn't throw your arms around me and kiss me passionately when I arrived last night. I guess it's not that easy to forget about being locked up behind barbed wire for nearly two years and pick up immediately where you left off without some hesitation and doubt. I promise to be more reasonable and try to cope with my new found freedom. Okay."

We sat for sometime in silence. I finally walked to the little alcove she called her kitchen, poured myself a scotch, came over and sat beside her, took her in my arms, and kissed her passionately. I withdrew, looked into her exquisitely beautiful eyes, and said, "I do love you, Mary, very much and we're getting married and that makes everything perfect so let's pick up where we left off. We can begin by having a bath together. Remember how wonderfully amorous they were. Besides, I sure need one."

We bathed together, made love, went to bed, made love, slept, woke, and made love again and I thought, *Gee, just like old times.*

With all Mary's free time, she and I spent a great deal of it in bed getting reacquainted. The awkward feeling we first experienced the first night together was gone. Our sexual compatibility picked up close to the point where it was before I was shot down. However, it never reached the intensity of those wonderful days and nights we spend together in the summer of 1943, most probably because of the constant danger I faced and knowing that it might be our last time together.

On Wednesday it finally dawned on us that we should think about a honeymoon and a place to stay besides Ivor Court after the marriage ceremony. Most of the resort hotels in the country were taken over by the military, so we decided to stay in London. Mary suggested the Dorchester Hotel on Park Lane, so we went to make reservations. We were shocked to learn that it was impossible to get any accommodations at all. The desk clerk at the Dorchester told us all the hotels in London were completely booked. Everyone that could get to the city wanted to be there to celebrate war's end. I pleaded my case, telling the hotel man that I had just gotten out of prison camp and we were getting married Saturday and had no place to stay. The clerk finally said, "I just can't help you. I wish I could. But let me call the assistant hotel manager. Perhaps he can be of some assistance."

When the manager arrived, I again went through my sad and woeful story again with Mary holding onto my arm like a poor damsel in distress.

After a prolonged discussion with the desk clerk, the manager finally said, "All right, why don't you plan to come here after the wedding and we'll have something for you. I can't promise much but I'm certain we'll find you and your lovely bride an accommodation."

We left the Dorchester after profusely thanking the hotel manager. Being very optimistic about our accommodations, Mary contacted her many friends, telling them of our wedding and inviting them to a reception at the Dorchester. I also met many of my buddies, mostly former POWs wandering around London, seeing their friends and visiting old haunts. On each occasion I'd introduce Mary, tell them about the wedding, and invite them to our reception, adding, "It's at one o'clock at the Dorchester. Please come and bring a bottle." Liquor was still rationed and was very difficult to get. We only had two bottles of scotch and a bottle of gin. By the number of people we had invited, it looked as if we were going to need a lot more. Hopefully, our guests would be generous.

Chapter 19

Late that afternoon when I returned from a walk in Regents Park, Mary told me she had called her mother to tell her that she was getting married and asked her if she would like to meet me. Mary had seen very little of her mother since she moved back to Hampstead in May 1940. Mary stayed in London and moved into a flat in Maida Vale with her friend Muriel.

Mary had a very sordid and abusive childhood. She was raised fatherless by a tyrannical mother who had physically and sexually abused her. Mary's infrequent visits to her mother over the past five years usually ended in an unpleasant and depressive meeting.

Mary told me, "My mother was very disagreeable and spiteful, and said, 'Don't bring that Yank over here because I don't want to meet him. You can go to America for all I care, but you'll be sorry and come crawling back to me, when he tires of you.'"

Mary tried again later that evening, thinking her mother had been drinking and would be sober and more congenial, but she got the same response.

Mary's friend Dorothy told Mary that she and Stephanos would be thrilled to stand up for her. They would have a dinner party for us after the wedding and Mary could invite anyone she wanted. Dorothy and Stephanos were with Mary the first night I met her. I had been in their company on several occasions in 1943 and Mary and I had dinner in their flat one evening. They were very fond of Mary.

My brother, Andy, was stationed, in England and had met Mary. He called her several months ago, shortly after he arrived at his duty station in Dorset and arranged to meet Mary in London. He arrived with his fiancée, Lieutenant Evelyn Smith, and they took Mary to dinner. She later visited them at their base near Shaftesbury. Andy was a captain in the Army Medical Corps.

Marry Me

I called Andy on Wednesday evening and told him I had returned and that Mary and I were getting married.

Andy responded enthusiastically, "That's really great, Bill. Congratulations! You're a lucky guy; we think Mary is terrific. Thank God you're back. Have you called Mother and Dad? They've been worried sick over you."

When I told him I'd wired home, Andy went on to say, "Let's meet for dinner tonight. How about the Grill Room? Okay? Great. I'll bring Ev. Wait until you meet her. She's quite a gal. You'll love her. Give Mary our love. See you at the Savoy."

We met in the lobby where Andy introduced Ev to me. She was a tall girl about the same height as Andy with short light brown hair, large blue eyes, and a very handsome face. Ev was from Kansas and she looked every bit the typical healthy, no-nonsense Midwestern girl. I liked her immediately.

Andy, not as tall as I, had dark brown hair and brown eyes and a full mustache. He was very much the extrovert. It had been more than four years since I had seen him and we had a lot of catching up. Andy pressed me, wanting to know all about my time as a POW and my combat tour. My answers were short and not too informative, I was more interested to know about our family — my mother and dad and our sisters.

Mary said very little, sitting back apparently enjoying the banter between Andy and me, and I was sure that she was somewhat surprised that we were so different. After much reminiscing and a fine dinner, Ev and Andy walked us to the hotel entrance where a taxi was waiting. They were staying at the Savoy, and as I followed Mary into the cab, Andy slapped me on the back and said, "I'll be back in London on Friday and help you through the ordeal, Bill."

Chapter 20

The Wedding

Andy arrived Friday night and he generously took us to dinner on the money I gave him to cover any wedding expenses. After dinner we took Mary back to Ivor Court. I wasn't too happy about leaving Mary because I wanted to be with her. But for appearance sake we decided that we could sacrifice one night when we had the rest of our lives to be together. Andy and I checked into the Jules Club, the Red Cross Club, on Jermyn Street where we had booked a room.

In the morning we arrived at Ivor Court at nine o'clock. Mary had arranged for her porter to pick up our uniforms and have them pressed while she was at Simpson's having her hair done. After the porter picked up our uniforms, I made some coffee and Andy insisted on lacing it with a shot of scotch. He said it would help me to get rid of the jitters. I hadn't slept that well wondering whether or not I was doing the right thing. So I guess I did look a little peeked. We opened one of the bottles and proceeded to have one and then another.

Mary came back to her flat at ten o'clock and we were still waiting for our uniforms. She dashed into the bathroom not wanting to see me before she was dressed for the wedding. When she heard the cork being removed from the bottle she called out, "You two, leave that scotch alone. That's all we have for the reception."

I looked at the half-empty bottle and, "Okay, babe, no more."

The porter returned our uniforms and when we were dressed, Andy said, "I have to pick up Ev at Paddington Station. We'll meet you and Mary at the Registry Office in Marylebone. Don't forget to give Mary the corsage I bought for her. Take good care of her, Bill. You're a lucky guy. See you at eleven." And to Mary in the bathroom he called out, "See you later, Mary. Don't be late."

Mary replied, "All right, Andy, and thanks for everything." Then to me, "Darling, do you mind waiting in the lobby for me while I finish dressing? I'll be there shortly."

"Okay, babe." I walked out with Andy. Twenty minutes later Mary entered the lobby. I looked up thinking, *God she's beautiful.*

She said, "I'm probably the first girl ever to get married in black. Do you mind?"

"Hell, no. You look terrific."

Mary spent much of the last three days rushing about London looking for something to wear for the wedding. Among other things, stylish dresses were very scarce and if found, required countless coupons. I told her to spend as much as she wanted and if she didn't have enough coupons, to get something on the black market. She refused and said positively not, she would buy her own dress. Then added, but after we're married, watch out. I'll expect a complete new wardrobe when we get to America. So she ended up buying a white silk blouse for three guineas, saying she could not find a thing she liked. So she wore her not-too-old black suit and the new silk blouse.

It was a few minutes before eleven when we got into the taxi for the short drive down the road to the Marylebone Registry Office. Mary was unusually quiet and I was my usual silent self, both of us sitting in the cab holding hands and looking very solemn. Andy and Ev, and Dorothy and Stephanos were waiting for us at the Registry Office. We were all invited in the office by an austere and sober-looking man also dressed in black.

The proceedings did not take long but it was indeed a very somber and serious ceremony. Mary appeared to be very subdued and quiescent, while I stood there in a hypnotic trance, not remembering one word that was said but managed to make the right responses at the appropriate time. During those few hectic days before the wedding, Mary saw and admired a platinum wedding band circled with diamonds in an estate jewelers in Knightsbridge. I went back to the store and bought it and now dutifully slipped it on Mary's finger. When we heard the registrar say, "I now pronounce you man and wife," I kissed her modestly. Then Mary broke from the traditional behavior of a bride by throwing her arms around my neck and kissing me tightly on my lips. Everyone laughed, even the sedate civil servant. She had changed the solemnity to a very happy and pleasant occasion. Everyone was smiling and there was a lot of hugging and kissing and I thought, *Well it hadn't been that painful after all.*

We walked out of the building and down the steps to the street. Andy dashed ahead to a large black limousine parked at the curb, held the door open, and said, "With my compliments, I borrowed it from the royal family." It did indeed look like the Austin Princess which the king and queen rode about in. It was a very pleasant surprise. Leave it to Andy to spare no expense, regardless of what it cost me. Mary and I happily got in and waved to the two couples standing on the sidewalk to begin our very uncertain future.

We picked up our sparse luggage at Mary's flat, where Andy and Ev planned to stay for the weekend, then proceeded to the hotel a short ten-minute drive down Gloucester Place to Park Lane. For an all-day-car hire it was very expensive and not at all practical, but it was certainly luxurious. We left the car, walked into the lobby, and up to the hotel clerk and asked with great apprehension, "Reservation for Captain and Mrs. Wheeler." It was the first time Mary had heard her new name and anxious as she was about our room, she looked very happy.

The desk clerk said, "One moment, please." He opened the reservation book while Mary and I stood desperately praying that he had a room for us. He finally said, "Yes, but of course. Here is your key and congratulations to you, Captain, and your lovely bride." And then to Mary, "Welcome to the Dorchester Hotel, Mrs. Wheeler. I trust you will find everything to your satisfaction. If not, please don't hesitate to let us know. Enjoy your stay."

I sighed deeply and thought, *that was a real impressive welcome*, took the key and thanked him graciously. I gave the key to the porter and followed him to the elevators. Mary energetically squeezed my arm and whispered, "Well, we do have a room. Thank God for that—after all the people we invited to our reception."

The porter took us to the fifth floor and guided us to the end of the corridor. He opened a door with a brass plaque on it. So anxious were we to see the room that we failed to notice the inscription on the door. The porter led us into a large foyer and from there into a very spacious reception room. It was magnificently decorated in off-whites and beautiful shades of blue. A deep plush, powder blue carpet covered the large floor. The tall floor-to-ceiling windows were draped in cream-colored satin. The chairs and sofas were done in rich brocade with matching ivory woodwork. It was truly the most elegant and sumptuous accommodations I had ever seen.

The porter turned to Mary and said, "May I show you the bedroom, madam?" He then led us into a room almost as large as the other, beautifully furnished in the same French Provincial decor. He placed our cases on the luggage rack and opened the drapes and the door to the bathroom.

The first thing that caught my eye was a huge oversized canopied bed. We both stood staring in awe, our hands tightly grasped together. When the porter had finished showing us the suite, he said, "Welcome to the Mountbatten Suite. Enjoy your stay with us."

I finally snapped out of my trance and handed the porter a pound note as he left the room. Mary rushed into my arms. We stood there holding each other for several minutes. Mary broke away and walked to the center of the room and picked up a card from a large, beautiful bouquet of roses displayed on a table behind the sofas. She read aloud the card to me, "Good Luck. Signed, Free. Oh, Bill, aren't they beautiful. I just can't believe that this lovely suite is for us. Isn't it wonderful and the flowers. We are truly, very fortunate."

She rushed back in my arms and kissed me firmly on the lips. I held her tight looking over her shoulder into the bedroom and that huge bed and said, "You bet. Let's get into that bed and spend our honeymoon there."

"Oh, Bill, you are a lecher. And you're right you know. I can't wait to get into it with you, but it's nearly one o'clock and we are having a reception, remember. We must order some hors d'oeuvres and you must set up the liquor, what little we have after you and Andy started to drink it this morning. If everyone comes that we've invited . . . I just hope they bring some whiskey with them. I'll call and order some food. Please don't expect too much because of the war. We're still rationed, you know."

To our amazement room service arrived with two huge silver trays of hors d'oeuvres. To Mary it was unbelievable, she hadn't seen that much food since before the war—delicacies like stuffed eggs, anchovies, sardines, cheeses, and much more.

Andy and Ev were first to arrive and they added a bottle of gin and brandy to our meager liquid supply. A short time later, a steady stream of guests arrived filling the large room to capacity. Most everyone brought something. My friends brought whiskey or gin and Mary's gave her pounds of sterling. She had told them that she did not want gifts because of the limited amount of luggage she could take by air to America. She received over two hundred pounds from her friends.

In spite of no planning and little preparation, the party was a huge success. Everything seemed to fall in place. There was more than enough liquor, in fact, there were six bottles left over. Mary found that the beautiful flowers were not from the hotel but from a Mrs. Freeman, a designer for whom she had modeled. My consumption of alcohol undoubtedly caused our first marital quarrel. Benny Newman, a friend of Mary's, brought a very attractive redhead named Penny, a show girl, with him to the reception. Penny made a play for the bridegroom and I, in a rather inebriated state, didn't discourage it. Mary was furious. We managed to keep our feelings somewhat in check until the last guest left. But at times her anger was hard to conceal and I knew that I was in for a real donnybrook.

When we were finally alone, Mary in no uncertain terms told me she did not appreciate my behavior and it better not happen again. An argument ensued and there was considerable doubt in both our minds about the longevity of our marriage. In fact, I'd serious doubts as to whether it would last through our four-day honeymoon at the Dorchester.

Mary was still seething with anger over my shameful behavior, when the phone rang. Mary answered the phone and after an awkward pause, she said, "Hello, Hal. Yes, won't you come up. I'd like you to meet Bill." She hung up, turned toward me, and said, "Hal McMillan is on his way up. I told you about him."

Before I had a chance to respond she picked up the phone, dialed room service, and said, "I'll order some tea." When she put the phone down she said, "I'm sorry, Bill, getting mad the way I did. I got very jealous when you were playing up to Penny. I'm sorry, all right?" She waited for me to reply and when I didn't, she added, "Hal called my flat and spoke to Andy who told him we were married and we were staying at the Dorchester. He said he wanted to meet you and wish us good luck." She hesitated for a moment, looked at me pleadingly, and said, "You will be nice to him. He was very good to me. I told you how he helped me through the measles."

Mary was visibly upset, although she had every intention of telling Hal about our marriage, she forgot to write to him. She knew he was away on a trip to America and she had intended to send the letter so he would get it when he returned to England. But with the excitement of my return and during those few hectic days in preparing for the wedding, she completely forgot. She felt very ashamed and upset.

I remained silent wondering how she was going to handle this situation. She broke the silence by saying, "Hal doesn't drink very much, so do you mind if we have tea."

"No."

The buzzer sounded and Mary opened the door. She took Hal's hand and led him into the room. Walking Hal toward me, she said, "Bill, this is Hal McMillan. Hal, I would like you to meet my...," she stopped, hesitated, and then continued, "Bill Wheeler."

We shook hands and I said, "Hi." He seemed much younger than me, slight of build, fair complexion, clean-cut, and rather handsome in a well-tailored air force uniform much better than my sack.

He returned my greeting and said he had heard a lot about me and knew that Mary was very happy that I was back. He told us he had just returned from the States. When he got to London and called Mary's flat he learned that we were married.

Initially my resentment was quite obvious and my responses were short and curt. The tea arrived and Mary busied herself serving us. The tension lessened somewhat and then surprisingly, I began to feel sorry for him. It was quite evident that he was very much in love with Mary and as hard as he tried to conceal it the disappointment and hurt showed plainly in his face. Mary managed to keep a fairly coherent conversation going and Hal joined her in a pleasant and polite dialogue.

When we finished tea, he said he had to leave. He took Mary's hand, held it, and said, "I wish you all the happiness you so rightfully deserve and the very best of everything. I know you are going to like America. Have a good save trip." He turned to me and held out his hand, saying, "Congratulations. Mary is a very remarkable and wonderful person. Take good care of her."

There was no doubt in my mind of the warmth and sincerity in his voice. I shook his hand firmly and said, "It was good meeting you, Hal. Thanks and good luck to you."

At the door Mary said goodbye and kissed him on the cheek. When he left she came into the room and stood quietly. When I saw the anguish in her face I went out onto the balcony, stood at the railing looking out at Hyde Park across Park Lane.

Mary came out, tucked her hand under my arm, and said, "I'm sorry, Bill. I did have every intention of telling him. I just plain forgot and I feel awful about it." She hesitated and then continued, "There was nothing serious between us. I told him about you and he knew that I would marry you when you came back." She stopped and then added, "But I should have written and told him that we were going to get married."

"Okay. I understand. But it was pretty obvious that the guy was crazy about you. He was hurt and I can't help feeling sorry for him."

Chapter 20

"Let's not talk about it anymore, Bill. You know we're going to dinner at the embassy at eight. It's going to be a long day. Can we have a *'little lie-down'*." An expression I well remember from those marvelous days and nights we spent together in 1943.

"Okay."

We went into the bedroom and Mary picked up a nightgown and disappeared into the bathroom. I undressed to my shorts and got into bed. Mary joined me a few minutes later. She snuggled up to me and I put my arm around her. So before a short nap, we indulged in our first legitimate sex and found it no different or better than our prior carnal couplings.

Later as we were leaving to join our party at the Embassy Club, I remembered the leftover tea cakes and wrapped them in a napkin and hid them in the bureau drawer. It would take me a while to forget the hunger I'd experienced in Germany and couldn't abide the thought of leaving the uneaten cakes.

Dorothy and Stephanos had invited us along with Andy and Ev and four close friends of Mary's to the Embassy Club for a wedding supper. We stopped on our way to thank the hotel manager who had somehow given us unbelievable accommodations. He said he was delighted that we liked the suite and told us it was one of the royal suites. Lord Mountbatten had stayed there on numerous occasions. Fortunately, no wedding party had been booked into the hotel that weekend so the suite was available. After hearing our desperate story, he was determined to find something for us. He said it made him very happy to be able to offer the suite to such a lovely young couple.

We left after thanking him repeatedly and were surprised to see the Austin Princess waiting under the portico. Andy had apparently briefed the driver to take us to the Embassy Club.

The wedding party at the club was first class. Again the whiskey and fine wine flowed generously. It was a very successful finish to our wedding day. Oscar and Renee, along with their wedding party, were also celebrating their marriage at the embassy. Theirs was hosted by Ann Taylor's friend, Jack Hylton, a well-known English bandleader.

Back in our spacious suite at the Dorchester, we wasted no time getting to bed. There, we talked about our wedding day and how wonderful it had been. Everything went so well. Probably not a wedding that most girls dreamed of but nevertheless it was a memorable and amazingly successful one for us. Mary's friends, particularly Dorothy, contributed much to making it a remarkable and happy occasion. Andy helped in many ways, most of all by just being there. Everything seemed to be orchestrated as if some divine presence had guided us through the day, making our wedding day perfect. Was it a good omen? Our conversation suddenly ended. We both became quiet and pensive. Had we rushed into our marriage too soon? I was sure, during my confinement, that I loved Mary and wanted to marry her. But now that I had, was I ready to assume the grave responsibility? I wasn't quite sure whether I was up to it. *Could I leave her alone and go to the Pacific as I had planned?* So many questions plagued me. I was no longer free to do as I pleased and must now think of someone besides myself. I remembered the words of the registrar—love, honor, and obey—but most important were the words I did not hear, which were to care for, trust, and protect. Was I capable of such an enormous and serious responsibility?

I was certain Mary too was filled with uncertainty. She had taken a giant plunge into marriage, cutting all ties and burning every bridge behind her—leaving England, her friends, and although not close, her mother and family. She had married me but knew that in some ways I had changed and was not the lover she knew before I was shot down. She was going to a strange country knowing no more about it than what she had seen portrayed by Hollywood. What about my family? She liked Andy for all his boastful ways, but what of my parents and sisters, would they accept her? There would be no one there for her to turn to or befriend her. She would be alone and completely dependent on me. Mary's marriage was a gutsy and challenging venture for her and hopefully she had the strength, faith, and love for me that would keep us together forever.

If Mary had any anxious fears and pessimistic thoughts she had put them aside. She snuggled up to me and buried her face in the hollow of my neck. I tightened my arms around her, pressing firmly against her, kissing the top of her head. It seemed important to get close—very close. We both were determined to declare our love for each other in the best and only way we knew. We made love eagerly, then languorously, consumed by a selfishness and conscientious greed for each other's body, knowing that our physical love would see us through any problems or differences we might face in the future. We were sure of that.

Later, during a lull between lovemaking and sleeping and suffering through my third hangover of the day, I remembered the stash of cakes hidden in the bureau drawer. While Mary rested, I retrieved my booty. I sat on the edge of the bed, stuffing myself with the deliciously rich cakes and warm milk, thinking of the countless nights, when lying on my palliasse in prison camp dreaming of this magnificent moment.

Chapter 21
Home at Last

My first priority after our wedding was to arrange passage for Mary to America. I was eager to get home to see my family and get back on flying status. As we were still at war with Japan, I felt it my duty to get back into the action. However, I didn't want another separation from Mary. I wanted to get her to America as soon as possible and preferably before I left for home.

The day we returned to Ivor Court, after three glorious nights at the Dorchester, I went directly to the Army Transportation Office behind Selfridges and was pleasantly surprised to find the officer in charge a Major Tom Barnaby from my home town. After the usual small talk about fellows we knew, I made the purpose of the visit known. "I got married last week to an English girl and I like to arrange passage for her to America."

He replied, "Bill, old buddy, get in line and put your name down. It will be a year to eighteen months to get your wife to the States."

Our friendship and no amount of persuasion on my part had any effect on him. He said there was absolutely nothing he could do about it. Feeling very exasperated and disappointed, I was determined to find a way to get Mary home before I left. The thought of leaving her in England was unbearable.

Chapter 21

Oscar was faced with the same problem and we set about to find a way to get passage for both Mary and Renee. We wined and dined every person we met that might possibly help us. I was desperate and after three futile weeks I went to Pan American Airways and begged the manager of the London office to sell me a ticket for Mary on the clipper to New York. He said, "Sure, I'll sell you a ticket for 250 pounds ($1,000) but you have to get your wife to Lisbon to make the connection." We bought the ticket after checking with British Airways who promised to get Mary to Lisbon, Portugal, if she could be ready to leave on two hours' notice. Mary didn't hesitate, but I had serious doubts about leaving her on her own without confirmed travel arrangements. And I'm sure she had certain reservations about giving up everything she owned, leaving London, her friends, and traveling alone to America. But she was determined. She sold the lease to her flat and disposed of all her furniture, personal property, and with only forty pounds of luggage and forty British pounds sterling (maximum amount she could take out of England) she moved into the Cumberland Hotel at Marble Arch.

The day after seeing me depart from Southampton on a troopship to Boston, Mary was called by British Airways informing her that a seat was available for her on a flight to Lisbon. She had two hours to get to Bournemouth to board a war-weary Dakota (DC-3). On the flight she met a young English woman, Julie Harris, on her way to America to marry a congressman from Illinois. They immediately became the best of friends and decided to room together when they arrived in Lisbon. There they moved into a suite in the finest hotel on the Estoril. They were devastated to learn that all flights on the clipper to America were booked solid for several weeks. After five days they had to scale down their accommodations when their limited funds expired. The hotel manager graciously let them stay until their promised funds arrived from England and America.

The morning of the seventh day while having breakfast Mary and Julie were jokingly discussing a man eating at the next table in what they believed to be his pajamas. He was obviously a foreigner so they spoke openly about the gentleman's attire. When they finished their breakfast and went to leave, the man stood and intercepted them and in a very distinct American accent said, "Excuse me, young ladies, this is a seersucker suit and it is not my pajamas." After an extremely embarrassing several minutes and an awkward introduction, he insisted that they join him for coffee. His name was Stanley Simons, an attractive man in his mid-forties who graciously accepted their apologies. After hearing of their travel problems of getting on the clipper and a lot about me and how anxious they were to get to New York, he agreed to help them. Two days later they were summoned to the terminal for their flight to the United States. Just before leaving the wired funds for Mary arrived and she had more money than she could legally take out of the country. She insisted that Mr. Simons take the excess funds and return it when they met in America.

After a day's delay at the Pentagon, I arrived home eleven days after leaving England. I was warmly greeted by my mother and father—and his first words were, "Bill, Pan Am just called and said that Mary had arrived and was waiting for you at LaGuardia." After a quick embrace from my parents my father handed me the keys to his car and said, "Better hurry, Bill."

I found Mary sitting on her pigskin trunk at the entrance to the terminal, holding a cup of tea and looking very distressed and lonely. She was dressed in an English tweed suit and needless to say she was sweltering on the first day of July in New York. However, she did look pleased when she saw me.

Two weeks later we were invited to Mr. Simons's home in Sutton Place in New York City. His wife was exceptionally beautiful and their home was magnificent. He returned the money that Mary had given to him and said to me, "Please caution your wife about giving money to strange men. It's not a very good idea."

I responded by saying under the circumstances, I thought it was a fine idea. Mr. Simons was a very prominent international lawyer and he was overseas representing Tiffany's.

Epilogue

Shortly after we returned to America I received one of the finest fitness reports from Colonel Darr Alkire I'd ever gotten in my entire military career. It commended me on my outstanding leadership, loyalty, and dedication as an air force officer under the most difficult conditions. It was a most rewarding commendation and made every adversity endured worthwhile. Unfortunately it could not be included in my military record as an official efficient rating because it covered a period of time that I was not under United States military control. But more importantly this most personal and valuable document was lost during our many travels and changes of duty stations. It would have been a most fitting ending to my story.